Why are you afraid?

Why are you afraid?

MICHAEL BUCKLEY

Darton, Longman and Todd
London

First published in Great Britain in 1979
by Darton, Longman and Todd Ltd
89 Lillie Road, London SW6 1UD

© 1979 Michael Buckley

All biblical quotations are from
The Jerusalem Bible
© 1966 Darton, Longman and Todd and Doubleday and Co Inc

ISBN 0 232 51444 5

Printed in Great Britain by The Anchor Press Ltd
and bound by Wm Brendon & Son Ltd, both of Tiptree, Essex

Contents

Acknowledgement

Thanks are due to the Mercier Press for permission to quote from *The God I Don't Believe In* by Julian Arias.

Introduction

Why write a book about fear? Recent events in my life
have given me insights into the destructive forces of fear
in our Church and society. We are all afraid in varying
degrees because basically we are a damaged people. Sin
has dealt us a crippling blow and we feel its insidious
presence numbing our capacity for self-determination.
We become mesmerized rabbits in the grip of stoatlike
fear from which we find it almost impossible to escape. It
helps us to break the psychological grip of fear when we
realize that Jesus himself suffered many crises of fear.
The divinization of Jesus has so stifled his humanity in
our understanding of him that we easily forget that his
agony in Gethsemane was 'for real' and not just an act
put on for our sake. *Jesus was afraid and nearly lost out*. If he
did – and there was always this possibility, if he was truly
human – then we could not even begin to hope to be
saved. His fear was so real that 'his sweat fell to the
ground like great drops of blood' (Luke 22:45). It is not a
sin to be afraid since fear is a result of our damaged
nature. When we are no longer afraid of being afraid we
can begin our conquest of fear. Just as the alcoholic has
to admit his alcoholism before he can be cured, so we
acknowledge our fear as the first step to changing the
direction of our lives towards God, our Father.

It takes courage to admit fear and to undertake tasks with a high risk of failure. Jesus nearly failed, but he didn't. Fear often blinds us not only to the possibility of success but to our own weaknesses. When we challenge fear then it engages us in an unbloody war with ourselves. Peter thought he was the bravest and most loyal of the apostles, but was he? His triple denial emphasises that his supposed strength was in fact his weakness. He damaged himself more than anyone else when fear challenged his faith. Fear won the first three battles, but faith won the war. Peter repented, and changed his attitude to Jesus and to himself, thus becoming not only the hero of the Early Church but of all time. Poor Judas was afraid to believe in forgiveness 'and went and hanged himself' (Matt. 27:5). Fear springs from the darkness, while faith looks to the light of Jesus who is our peace and reconciliation. His Spirit will so heal us from the domination of fear that we will realise that weakness is part of our human condition. Fear tells us that once we have failed we will never succeed; faith assures us that while there is life, there is always hope in him who is our strength.

We are not, then, to be afraid of failure. It is far too easy to follow a gospel or way of life which has an in-built guarantee of perpetual and unqualified success. We have to take up our cross and walk in his footsteps knowing that we cannot avoid the pain out of which victory is born. I now know more than at any time in my priestly life that prophecy sometimes means a calling out into the desert, with the mocking of our own echo as our only response, which haunts us with apparent failure and loneliness. Today we need Christian voices to proclaim his kingdom to a parched world which has not yet received the life-giving rain of the gospel. The world has not listened before but it will listen now if, like Peter after his denial when he met the Risen Lord, we remember that our nets will be filled only at Jesus's word and under his direction:

Simon Peter said, 'I'm going fishing'. They replied, 'We'll come with you'. They went out and got into the boat but caught nothing that night. It was light by now and there stood Jesus on the shore, though the disciples did not realise that it was Jesus. Jesus called out, 'Have you caught anything, friends?' And when they answered, 'No', he said, 'Throw the net out to starboard and you'll find something'. So they dropped the net and there were so many fish that they could not haul it in. (John 21:3–6)

We are not afraid of failure. The Peace People of Northern Ireland took to the streets when everything seemed so hopeless. In hindsight observers said it happened to be the right time, but the answer is not as simple as that. They met a need, born out of despair, and through their courage people began to hope again. They lit a flame from which others have kindled their torches of peace and hope. Their success cannot be measured in political terms but it is certain that Northern Ireland will never be the same again. A new dimension of faith scaled the forbidding walls of fear and those who shared the vision with the brave women of peace saw the new Jerusalem as it might and will be. Those who marched for peace in Northern Ireland not only crossed frontiers within themselves but were also helped by each other's presence to find new courage, to dare to dream of things that might be, if only they were prepared to pay the price for them. The inspiration of this book came from my brave friends in Northern Ireland who lifted up our eyes to new horizons and gave strength to wearied pilgrims' feet. Peacemaking is only for the brave, who know what it is to conquer fear within themselves because they are prepared to acknowledge their own human frailty, both in motivation and action.

There are so many things of which we are afraid. We talk a great deal, for example, about Christian unity, but as soon as the Churches are brought too close for comfort then all the hidden attitudes and prejudices begin to surface. We wish to avoid the challenge and confrontation of unity and so withdraw to our entrenched positions where we feel safe. Those who attempt to pioneer the path to unity as scouts for the main body to which they belong will soon discover that they are regarded as 'deserters' who have gone over to the other side. The points of difference between the Churches have come to be regarded as so essential as to become the criteria of orthodoxy. As Churches we are afraid of Christian unity and we are afraid to say so. The charade continues under the banner whose motto is 'hasten slowly' (*festina lente*), and the urgency of the gospel is forgotten.

In many ways we are so frightened within the Churches that we are afraid to make peace which is the basis of unity. We refuse to compromise on the 'essential inessentials', so that our distrust of each other is greater than the intimidation of physical violence. What is true of Northern Ireland is also true of this country once we put all our cards on the table. Is our attitude in England towards the inessentials of faith any different from those whom we pharisaically condemn as bigoted? We are still being told in these islands, where we suffer not so much from bigotry but from tolerance bordering on apathy, that it is a 'serious sin' not to send our children to a Catholic school. But is this true in all circumstances? Indeed the reverse may be true. 'For if men use the green wood like this, what will happen when it is dry?' (Luke 23:31).

We are often afraid to be Christian because we are too Catholic or too Protestant, depending on our upbringing and environment. We are afraid to stand up and be counted for the Christian faith. Northern Ireland has taught me how Christian and forgiving so many people can be, despite the pressures on them from both secular and ecclesiastical society to remain polarized. The bravery and faith of the new emerging Church is a challenge to us all. I have received from people in Northern Ireland the extra spur to realize that 'small is beautiful', and that the individual can never be conquered if his belief in the power of the Spirit rules his life. Fear tells us that we can never change the system. Faith encourages us to be different and reminds us that systems are unimportant in relation to people.

Our greatest task will always remain that of conquering within ourselves. We have to face up to who we are and come to terms with the weaknesses as well as the potential which make up the real 'me'. We have to love ourselves as we are because otherwise we will start life as defeated people. We are a *victorious* people in Jesus Christ, who has conquered sin, death and the world. We can, and we shall, do all things in the power of him who died and rose for us. We are a chosen people and we have a right to claim our inheritance *now*.

We are nothing less than the children of God, whose life we share since he is our Father. No one can take our freedom from us which we receive through the liberating power of the gospel. Jesus wants us to be fully human and fully alive. If we love ourselves as God loves us then, and only then, will we begin to really love our neighbour. Love of self in its true sense is the key which unlocks the door to life. When we step out into the light and refuse to be intimidated by fear then for us a new dawn with a zest for living will have begun. We will live by the power given to us by the Spirit and not remain a puppet on a string. We will be free from the domination of fear and free to live as Christians.

Michael Buckley
Feast of St David, 1979.

1. Were you afraid, Lord?

Jesus was not immune from fear. If he were, then he would be less than human since fear is part and parcel of our damaged human nature. Jesus is one with us precisely because he is a man. St Paul in his writings constantly reminds us that Jesus so identified himself with our human condition that he was like us in everything but sin. Jesus was, like you and me, subject to all the weaknesses and temptations of a humanity alienated from God. He was subjected to fear and it is a great help to us to understand how he reacted to it. He did not find it easy and neither will we.

He was surrounded during his lifetime, from his birth to his death, by people who largely because of him were victims of obsessive fears. Jerusalem was a city of rumour and intrigue. The people's religion had become horribly mixed up with politics. Jesus was trapped between synagogue and state. His words were open to misinterpretation especially when he spoke of 'freedom' or 'a kingdom'. Jesus was caught up in the vortex of violence and fear which such a situation breeds. It was as if his life had unlocked the forces of evil.

Even though Jesus's 'kingdom' was not of this world, Herod because of him had innocent children slaughtered in order to protect his throne. Jesus preached 'freedom' to a people who lived not so much under the yoke of Roman Imperialism as under the burden of bigotry and observance of petty religious laws. Caiaphas, who was a politician rather than a priest, saw the danger inherent in a situation where the crowds followed the preacher from Nazareth:

> Then the chief priests and Pharisees called a meeting. 'Here is this man working all these signs,' they said, 'and what action are we taking? If we let him go on in this way everybody will believe in him, and the Romans will come and destroy the Holy Place and our nation.' One of them, Caiaphas, the high priest that year, said, 'You don't seem to have grasped the situation at all; you fail to see that *it is better for one man to die for the people** than for the whole nation to be destroyed'. He did not speak in his own person, it was as high priest that he made this prophecy that Jesus was to die for the nation – and not for the nation only, but to gather together in unity the scattered children of God. From that day they were determined to kill him. *So Jesus no longer went about openly among the Jews*, but left the district for a town called Ephraim, in the country bordering on the desert, and stayed there with his disciples. (John 11: 47-54)

It was to avoid being killed that Jesus had to alter his plans. However, once he was captured and brought before Caiaphas, the high priest repeated his prophecy: 'It is better for one man to die for the people' (John 18:14), thus showing that Jesus was expendable. It is strange how religious institutions can rationalize their actions once they are threatened. The death of Jesus was the lesser of two evils.

Jesus evoked feelings of hatred among his own people in Nazareth when he preached in his home-town synagogue:

---

* Author's italics here and throughout biblical quotations.

They sprang to their feet and hustled him out of town; and they took him up to the brow of the hill their town was built on, intending to throw him down the cliff, but he slipped through the crowd and walked away. (Luke 4: 29–30)

The Prince of Peace seemed to touch off hidden forces of bigotry and frustration everywhere, and it was in his beloved Jerusalem that the people in the city for a religious feast suddenly disintegrated into a rabble shouting for his blood. It was a straightforward choice – Jesus or Barabbas – peace or violence. He had only preached peace and a rabble always chooses violence. They were all afraid, from Pilate and the Sanhedrin down to the man in the street, of whom he might be – 'so you are a king then?' – and of what he might do – 'he said he would destroy the temple'. Their fears played on his words so that everything was twisted at his trial. Fear won the day when they crucified peace on a hill called Golgotha. His blood was truly on them and on their children.

During the period of his shameful trial and humiliation even his own followers, with the exception of Peter, were nowhere to be seen because they were afraid for their own skins. It was not that they loved him less but that they loved themselves more. I am sure that they had a good explanation for their actions in the moment of crisis when everything came unstuck in a way which they least expected. Peter, usually so loyal, who had proved himself 'brave' enough to assault a Roman soldier, was scared by a serving-girl into denying him. The only ones to remain loyal were a young boy and the women who had followed him during his public ministry. The unique figure among them was Mary, his mother, who stayed with him right to the end. In her we see the true living representation of a love which overcomes fear. The mother in this case did not abandon her first-born.

From the moment he was captured by the soldiers

3

until his death, Jesus was the most calm and controlled person amid all the ugly scenes that shook Jerusalem to the foundations. It was as if alone among leaders of state and religion he preserved his dignity and sense of purpose. What kept him going when ordinary people would have cracked under the strain? Was he showing himself to be a God who was not affected by puny people with their frustrating fears who were looking for a scapegoat? The answer, quite simply, is that he was showing himself to be a *man of faith* who had come face to face with fear within himself and had conquered it. After his agony in the Garden of Gethsemane he was ready for anything that people could do to him. He was no longer afraid.

He conquered fear the night before in a garden. The trial of Jesus began and ended in Gethsemane. There he had reached his decision and found peace within himself. It will help us to understand his inner power of peace when we examine in some detail the circumstances of his encounter with himself in the darkness of a garden. Jesus had all the symptoms of someone under great stress and one could describe him as being on the verge of a nervous breakdown. He was tempted to throw in the towel and cede victory to the massive forces arraigned against him. He could not win, and the thought must have occurred to him to slip away from all the violence and wait for a more opportune time to preach his message when things would have quietened down. In the meantime he could carry on his wonderful work of healing. After all he was only thirty-three years of age with a lifetime before him. This form of rationalizing, while human, did not take into account his Father's will. In prayer he learns more clearly what has to be and he surrenders lovingly. This was his moment of crisis and the moment of truth.

In him we all see ourselves as we grapple with the problems of faith and fear. We compare our problems with his. We, too, have to ask ourselves the question why we are placed under stress and tensions in particular situations. 'Why us, Lord?' we ask. Jesus is a man in agony who has finally arrived at a crunch situation and in the time of trial his faith in God his Father comes shining through. He told his captors, 'This is your hour; this is the reign of darkness' (Luke 22:53). In fact it was his glorious hour when faith conquers fear and light overcomes the darkness. We will never conquer fear or come to know ourselves unless we pray. Fear comes to us all. It is in prayer that the great decisions in life are taken, once we allow faith to cancel out fear. What Jesus has done, we know that in faith we can do. We are never alone when we turn to God in prayer and in him we find our new strength.

Here is how Matthew's gospel describes the 'crisis situation':

Then Jesus came with them to a small estate called Gethsemane; and he said to his disciples, 'Stay here while I go over there to pray'. He took Peter and the two sons of Zebedee with him. And sadness came over him, and great distress. Then he said to them, 'My soul is sorrowful to the point of death. Wait here and keep awake with me.' And going on a little further he fell on his face and prayed. *'My Father,' he said 'if it is possible, let this cup pass me by. Nevertheless, let it be as you, not I, would have it.'* He came back to the disciples and found them sleeping, and he said to Peter, 'So you had not the strength to keep awake with me one hour? You should be awake, and praying not to be put to the test. The spirit is willing but the flesh is weak.' Again, a second time, he went away and prayed: 'My Father' he said 'if this cup cannot pass by without my drinking it, your will be done!' And he came back again and found them sleeping, their eyes were so heavy. Leaving them there, he went away again and prayed for the third time, repeating the same words. Then he came back to the disciples and said to them, 'You can sleep

5

on now and take your rest. Now the hour has come when the Son of Man is to be betrayed into the hands of sinners. Get up! Let us go! My betrayer is already close at hand.' (Matt. 26:36–46)

Because he was afraid and under pressure Jesus took three of his closest followers with him to keep him company. It is easier to overcome fear when you have someone to whom you can talk who understands you. We need the comforting contact of friends even if it is only to know that they are physically near us. They may be able to offer no other kind of help, because basically the problem within us can only be solved by ourselves alone. No one can solve our really big problems for us. We have to face up to our crisis ourselves and grow from it as real persons. I know that in any crisis of my life, it is when I gave myself time and space to reflect and pray that I found the answer which had always been there deep within myself. The most difficult person to live with is oneself and it takes a lifetime to understand the real self.

So it was with Jesus in Gethsemane. It was a time of trial: 'and sadness came over him and great distress'. We discover who we really are in moments of great joy or deep sorrow. They are sent to make us grow as real people. Jesus shared his crisis with those whom he could really trust. He confided in them which meant he hoped that they would understand what he was going through: 'My soul is sorrowful to the point of death.' He was so distressed that his sorrow overpowered him, a typical example of someone who sees no way out of the dilemma in which he finds himself. Is this the end or only the beginning? In fact while it was near the end of his own physical life, it was only the beginning of his glorious new life in the world. When everything else is lost we discover ourselves in a new way. It is when we think we have lost God that we are most near to finding and being found by him.

6

All Jesus asked of his closest friends was: 'Wait here and keep awake with me.' They were his 'moral' support. If Jesus was willing to depend on others, then surely we should not be too proud to ask for the help of others in times of need. Even though we have to solve the problem ourselves and make the decision alone, it is encouraging to know that others care about what happens to us. Jesus had spent his whole public life helping others and now it was his turn to receive their help. It is important to realize that it is blessed to receive as well as to give. Jesus proved that he was fully human by his urgent plea for assistance while he sorted out his future in prayer.

Our world may be justly criticized for many of its faults, but I have found genuine concern among Christians who are only too willing to share our load in time of trial. Peter, James and John were there in the garden to help Jesus carry his cross and this sharing has been the mark of the true followers of the Master all down through the centuries. We learn to share both our joys and our sorrows and so prevent ourselves from being isolated. Jesus in Gethsemane was lonely without being isolated. The feeling of isolation is destructive of ourselves and of those round us when we refuse to receive help.

Jesus had his great moment of joy some time before which far exceeded his triumphant entry into Jerusalem the previous Sunday: it was the Transfiguration:

Six days later, Jesus took with him Peter and James and his brother John and led them up a high mountain where they could be alone. There in their presence he was transfigured: his face shone like the sun and his clothes became as white as the light. Suddenly Moses and Elijah appeared to them; they were talking with him. Then Peter spoke to Jesus. 'Lord', he said 'it is wonderful for us to be here; if you wish I will make three tents here, one for you, one for Moses and one for Elijah.' He was still speaking when suddenly a bright cloud covered them with shadow, and from the cloud there came a voice which said, 'This is my Son, the Beloved; he enjoys my favour. Listen to him.' When they heard this *the disciples fell on their faces, overcome with fear. But Jesus came up and touched them. 'Stand up,' he said 'do not be afraid.'* And when they raised their eyes they saw no one but only Jesus. (Matt. 17:1–8)

He shared his joy on that occasion also with Peter, James and John but it was their turn to be afraid. He encouraged them, 'Do not be afraid' and touched them. By his human 'contact' he brought reassurance, but now in Gethsemane the roles were reversed: *they were there for him*. When we share our joys with others they will be better equipped to share our sorrows as well. Unfortunately we do not share our joys as much as we should and, while we mourn with the mourner, we do not find it as easy to rejoice with those who are joyful. When faith is always sad there is something amiss. We are a joy-filled people who when the going is hardest remember the good times. If we are grateful for those things which lift us up when we are low, then we are discovering a power for hope within us. God who has been faithful in the past will never abandon us.

Jesus begins to pray: 'My Father,' he said 'if it is possible, let this cup pass me by. Nevertheless, let it be as you, not I, would have it.' The prayer of Jesus is a prayer of faith. He knew all his life that God believed in him but now it was his turn to believe totally in God. He did not see the answer nor a way out of the situation in which he found himself. He was prepared, however, to surrender everything including his life. He did not want to die. 'If it is possible', but his trust in God is absolute: 'Let it be as you, not I, would have it.' We often pray, 'my will be done and yours only when it coincides with mine'. In this way we are not praying the prayer of faith; the prayer of someone who places God's will at the centre of his thoughts.

Jesus was Father-orientated. Even in the midst of all his anxiety God was still his Father. God's ways are not ours and we do not know all the answers. We hand over our fears to God believing and trusting in his loving purpose for us. The dynamic force directing the life of Jesus was his love for his Father and for us whom he was redeeming: a love 'that looks on tempests and is never shaken'. A loving faith does not always have a ready answer, but is prepared to listen to God who will provide the answer. Faith which has all the answers is no faith at all. Abraham did not have the answer when he climbed the mountain prepared to sacrifice his son Isaac; that is why he is called 'our father in faith'. When Isaac asked his father the question: 'Here are the fire and the wood, but where is the lamb for the burnt offering?' Abraham answered, 'My son, God himself will provide the lamb for the burnt offering' (Genesis 22:7–8). God did provide the offering in the person of his only Son. Jesus in Gethsemane is our brother in faith, and those who say he knew all the answers to his life would detract from his living faith which still called God 'my Father' in the agony of his greatest trial.

Jesus needed all the faith he could muster during his 'crisis' and when he was put to the test he was not found wanting. Theologians in the past have not stressed sufficiently the humanity of Jesus nor highlighted enough his faith as an example to us all. Too often they so over-emphasised his divinity that they almost ignored his humanity, thus defeating the whole purpose and meaning of the Incarnation. Jesus has often been depicted as 'too holy to be real' or else made into such a superman that his way of life completely transcends ours. In this false approach to Jesus we forget that he is one of us and we tend so completely to identify him with God that he is God and nothing else. I am afraid this way of thinking

9

was drilled into me at school and it takes a long time to get out of it. I now believe that Jesus as a man had very special personal faith through his open response to his Father. He loved God with a total human love.

'Yahweh has been pleased to crush him with suffering.' (Isa. 53:10). Suffering for me only has meaning when we grow in love because of it. Sometimes I do not understand suffering but I accept it in faith, believing that God my Father is sending it to me because he loves me. It was this approach to God which helped Jesus to face all the agony of his rejection and crucifixion. If one can use the words loosely, he came through his sufferings 'a better man'. He probably did not grasp the full significance of his agony but he was willing to undergo it because of love which gave depth to his living faith.

This emphasis on a living faith is much more real as well as being more relevant to us than any ill-founded piety which would depict Jesus as someone who knew everything always. If this were the case, then to what purpose was all the suffering in the garden of Gethsemane? It would have been a 'sham' with no meaning for us, as if Jesus were saying to himself, 'This will soon be over and so for a little while I shall just have to grin and bear it.' This minimizing of Jesus's faith is destructive of the gospels which accepted the *full humanity* of the person before their eyes. John knew about whom he was writing:

Something which has existed since the beginning,
that we have heard,
and we have seen with our own eyes;
that we have watched
and touched with our hands;
the Word, who is life –
this is our subject.
That life was made visible:

10

we saw it and we are giving our testimony. (1. John 1:1–2)

What was the extent of Jesus's fear? We will never know but we can say that despite his fear he won through as a man. He could without sin have refused to die. So many people think quite wrongly that he could not have done anything else but obey because he was God. This is quite false. As a man he was so in love with his Father and us that he was prepared to undergo anything, whatever the cost to himself. He was free. He had no 'special aids' to see him through and so he was just like you and me in our trials and sufferings. He has conquered fear in himself and invites us to do the same. He calls to us from beyond the grave. 'I love you so much that I was prepared to die for you. I gave my life so that you might come alive in me and I in you. I know what it feels like to be tempted to throw in the towel but please remember I am with you in your agony, as you were with me in the garden in my mind and heart. I went through my indecision and my crisis and my victory is your hope. Keep your eyes fixed on me. Whatever you may suffer I have been there before you. Come, follow me.'

Time and again in his public life Jesus demanded total dedication from his followers: 'If anyone wants to be a follower of mine, let him renounce himself and take up his cross every day and follow me. For anyone who wants to save his life will lose it; but anyone who loses his life for my sake, that man will save it. What gain, then, is it for a man to have won the whole world and to have lost or ruined his very self?' (Luke 9:23–5). He never compromised on the hardships of following him:

As they travelled along they met a man on the road who said to him, 'I will follow you wherever you go'. Jesus answered, 'Foxes have holes and the birds of the air have nests, but the Son of Man has nowhere to lay his head'.

11

Another to whom he said 'Follow me', replied, 'Let me go and bury my father first'. But he answered, 'Leave the dead to bury their dead; your duty is to go and spread the news of the Kingdom of God'.

Another said, 'I will follow you, sir, but first let me go and say goodbye to my people at home'. Jesus said to him, 'Once the hand is laid on the plough, no one who looks back is fit for the kingdom of God'. (Luke 9:57–62)

That night in the garden he had the sons of Zebedee with him. It was in a sense ironic that they were there since previously their mother had approached Jesus, as one would expect mothers to do, and asked for preferment for her sons:

Then the mother of Zebedee's sons came with her sons to make a request of him, and bowed low; and he said to her, 'What is it you want?' She said to him, 'Promise that these two sons may sit one at your right hand and the other at your left in the kingdom'. 'You do not know what you are asking' Jesus answered. 'Can you drink the cup that I am going to drink?' They replied, 'We can'. 'Very well,' he said 'you shall drink my cup, but as for seats at my right hand and my left, these are not mine to grant; they belong to those to whom they have been allotted by my Father.' (Matt. 20:20–23)

In Gethsemane the boot was now firmly on the other foot. Jesus was faced with the question of how much he loved his Father. He had asked total love of others so it was now up to him. He was to prove himself the perfect leader who followed his own instruction. He still asked: 'If it is possible, let this chalice pass from me.' The chalice, however, did not pass from him and he had to drink it to the dregs. We too in our lives preach the gospel of total love and faith in God, but there come

12

times of crisis when we are put to the test. A whole lifetime often finds its climax in a single decision affecting our faith. I know literally hundreds of people in my pastoral experience who have given up everything to follow Jesus. They turned their backs on wealth and security, the prospect of a happy marriage, or a way of life which ran counter to their faith. Their response was total surrender. This is the stuff of which saints are made. They are our cloud of witnesses in heaven and on earth of the power of faith against all odds. They gave up everything for faith which was their precious jewel for which they sold everything. Now perhaps we will pray more deeply for an increase of faith and say with more meaning the words of the Lord's prayer, 'do not put us to the test'.

The test of faith for Jesus came that evening in Gethsemane. His faith was being built up over the years which would equip him to deal with his moment of trial. So too in our own experience we find that our faith life of years is being tested in a situation perhaps not of our own making. We can pray, like Jesus, for the chalice to pass if it be possible, but when it is not possible we lovingly accept the decision with all its consequences. 'Faith is that', says Metropolitan Anthony Bloom, 'for which we are prepared to die because without it life would not be worth living.' Fear has no power over us once we are prepared to live a life of faith which even death itself cannot conquer. If we live faith-filled lives there is no room in our spirits for fear.

When Jesus returned to his disciples he 'found them sleeping, their eyes were so heavy'. They had, in a sense, failed him and so Jesus comes to his decision alone before his Father. Jesus tells us, by his example, that no one can solve the problems that trouble the deepest parts of our soul, but God alone in our encounter with him. No one can solve another's problems which touch the 'deep', the inner soul of a person's conscience. It is only God who shows us the way to an authentic answer. The building

13

up of conscience is one of the most vital functions facing us as Christians today. We cannot say we are obeying orders unless they are from God, our Father.

Each one must go through his agony while the closest to him can only watch and pray. In moments of trial for others when they are faced with the knowledge that they are seriously ill or have suffered a bereavement, we are one with them in prayer that they will come through their trial with dignity and courage. Like Jesus who said to Peter, 'I have prayed for you that your faith will not fail you', we pray that their belief in God's power to help them will never waver. Sometimes we have to stand by and watch them struggle within themselves in their agony when faith and fear are locked in combat. It costs us dearly when we know ourselves to be so helpless to 'do' anything. How much more tragic when those in a crisis of suffering have little or no faith on which to draw. This is to me the supreme tragedy. It seems a meaningless agony with little or no sign of any maturing of the person on trial. Suffering is necessary for us to grow in an awareness of ourselves and, where there is no faith, then suffering is indeed futile. It is like planting vines in a desert.

Jesus rises up from prayer and is completely at peace within himself. He has come to terms with suffering and is prepared for whatever is still to come. He has been through the valley of darkness so what evil should he fear? God is with and in him. He is refreshed and invigorated with new strength to face his enemies who are close at hand. 'You have prepared a banquet for me in the sight of my foes' (Ps. 23). Jesus loves his Father and any love worth the name involves suffering. When we come through our pain we will view the world and everything in it in a new light. It was as if before we were only half seeing people and things but, when we look from the hilltop of faith beyond the valley of suffering, we will have a clearer and more far-reading vision. This is always the case with the people of faith who have suffered.

Jesus from now on throughout his trial and death has a mysterious calmness and courage which is difficult for his enemies to understand. He had died completely to himself in the garden and his peace of soul is something which no one can take from him. It was as if when the Roman soldiers beat him in the courtyard they were battering futilely at a stout door which would not yield. His silence before the priests was more than an eloquent defence; it was a hymn of praise for his Father who he knew could deliver him. He walked in the light of his Father's love. It is not surprising that the Roman centurion who saw many criminals die on a cross screaming for mercy or vengeance realised that Jesus was different: 'In truth this man was a Son of God' (Mark 15:39). Jesus lived a new life, as it were, after his agony in the garden. He had been through his trial within himself and with God: a trial of hate by men, however gruesome in its details, was nothing by comparison. Jesus was truly alive and his love shone clearly on those around him if only they would look. The soldiers could kill his body: his soul belonged to his Father. We too can have this serenity once we rid ourselves of fear. If we come alive to God, then we will die to fear within ourselves which is the selfishness that clings to shadows.

When Jesus rose from the dead his message to his followers was one of peace. He repeated his advice to them time and again, 'do not be afraid'. He knew what fear was and the crisis he had to suffer. He had surrendered himself and his life to his Father. When we are in our agony we may ask him: 'Were you afraid, Lord?' He will answer: 'Yes, and I conquered it. Like death it has no sting. I am with you now. I am praying for you that your faith will not fail you. When you win through you will stand by my side and together we will bury fear forever.'

2. Peter, why were you afraid to stand up and be counted?

Fear is a most destructive force. It makes us look on people as a threat rather than a gift. It is the poison of Iago which pours distrust into the mind and heart of Othello. Fear affects the whole structure of society from the individual within the family to nations which live in an uneasy peace with each other. Where fear rules then man obeys the laws of the jungle. Envy, lack of self-confidence, dread of failure, sense of inferiority, feelings of insecurity are the side effects of the disease of fear. We are diseased – not at ease – within ourselves and we spread the contagion to all those with whom we come in contact. Fear and ignorance become a rapid breeding ground which spills over into hate of such an intense ferocity as we have witnessed in our time in Cyprus, Lebanon, Northern Ireland, Palestine, Rhodesia and many other places in our world. We are caught in the grip of fear and it refuses to let go so that today we live in a violent world. The atom bomb of fear has exploded in our midst and the whole world is suffering from its deadly fall-out. Fear has bedevilled industry and politics and even religious sects cannot shake off its tentacles. Christian unity, for example, would be brought about much more quickly if the various denominations trusted each other more instead of looking over the emotional wall of distrust at what the other side is doing.

Much of what is good in our lives never sees the light of day because of fear. Even in the human body the destructive effects of fear are seen. Stage fright can inhibit speech so that our minds are paralysed. The story is told of an amateur theatrical production in which the young man has to go on the stage and say just one line to the damsel in distress running away from her wicked uncle. The words were simple – 'flee to my lodge on the hill'. After weeks of rehearsal the opening night came and the young man rushed on to the stage and shouted in a voice cracking with emotion – 'lodge with my fleas on the hill'. He stopped the show and it was minutes before the dramatic atmosphere could be restored. Things can easily inhibit us so that we become like rabbits mesmerised by the stoat. A microphone put in front of us makes us go hot and cold so that the voice which comes forth from our throats is scarcely recognisable; that is if we can speak at all. The recurrent nightmare for us is one in which our legs turn to cotton wool as we become powerless to run away from the source of the threat. From primeval times we have feared the dark and the 'things that go bump in the night'.

The worst kind of fear is the one which affects our spirit. It prevents us from doing the things we know we should do so that we have not the moral courage to stand up and be counted. People and situations can threaten us so that we become inhibited in spirit and never become our real selves. It is only when we live the lives that deep in our innermost being we know we should be living, that we discover true happiness of spirit. We are at one with ourselves. There is then a harmony in our lives through which, despite the troubles round us, we learn to live at peace with ourselves. However, there come moments through pressure, intimidation or weakness when we fail

17

ourselves and it is at such times that not only must we forgive ourselves but also learn from the situation. We grow through our mistakes if we honestly analyse them and see ourselves as we really are.

We think we know our weaknesses yet we sometimes fail in those matters which we have long considered to be our strength. The danger is that when we fail once in our strong suit we will capitulate completely and throw in our hand. Such an attitude is fatal and fatalistic. We know that Peter disowned Jesus and Judas betrayed him, yet whose was the greater sin? We treat Peter with love as the Head of the Apostles while poor Judas is considered to be the epitome of evil. I have always had great compassion for Judas and believe that the Lord will treat him more kindly than we have. The great difference in history between Peter and Judas is that Peter lived on to achieve great things for the kingdom, whereas Judas could not live with his betrayal. Peter was repentant and hoped for forgiveness; Judas was remorseful and condemned himself. We will never know what wonderful things Judas would have done for the Lord if only he had forgiven himself. He is remembered as the apostle who 'lost out' because he gave in to despair. Despair is lack of hope – a fatalism that we are doomed come what may – and is the coffin in which fear buries us. One of the most attractive virtues in the Church is that, while it condemns sin, it forgives the sinner however grievous his faults. I hope that in the future it will speak more positively and forgivingly about Judas.

The events surrounding Peter's denial of his Master help us to understand that 'once down is no battle'. Peter is widely acknowledged as the apostle of faith. He was given the name Peter or rock (*petra*) because of his unshakable faith in the godhead of Jesus:

When Jesus came to the region of Caesarea Philippi he put this question to his disciples, 'Who do people say the Son of Man is?' And they said, 'Some say he is John the Baptist, some Elijah, and others Jeremiah or one of the prophets'. 'But you' he said 'who do you say I am?' Then Simon Peter spoke up, 'You are the Christ,' he said 'the Son of the living God'. Jesus replied, 'Simon, son of Jonah, you are a happy man! Because it was not flesh and blood that revealed this to you but my Father in heaven. So I now say to you: You are Peter and on this rock I will build my Church. And the gates of the underworld can never hold out against it. I will give you the keys of the kingdom of heaven: whatever you bind on earth shall be considered bound in heaven; whatever you loose on earth shall be considered loosed in heaven'. (Matt. 16:13–19)

Peter's faith in Jesus was his outstanding virtue and it came as a great shock to him when his Master prophesied that the apostle would disown him.

The prophecy concerning Peter's denial took place after the institution of the eucharist when the new covenant was celebrated. Everything that happened at the Last Supper was full of meaning and emotion so that the most unlikely event that could be envisaged was Peter's denial. Yet that was how it worked out down to the last detail. It will help us to understand the enormity of Peter's fall when we put the two events of prophecy and fulfilment in juxtaposition:

Then Jesus said to them, 'You will all lose faith in me this night, for the scripture says: I shall strike the shepherd and the sheep of the flock will be scattered, but after my resurrection I shall go before you into Galilee'. At this *Peter said, 'Though all lose faith in you, I will never lose faith'. Jesus answered him, 'I tell you solemnly, this very night, before the cock crows, you will have disowned me three times'.* Peter said to him, 'Even if I have to die

19

with you, I will never disown you'. (Matt. 26:30–5)

Peter was sitting outside in the courtyard, and a servant-girl came up to him and said, 'You too were with Jesus the Galilean'. But he denied it in front of them all. 'I do not know what you are talking about,' he said. When he went out to the gateway another servant-girl saw him and said to the people there, '*This man was with Jesus the Nazarene*'. *And again, with an oath, he denied it, 'I do not know the man*'. A little later the bystanders came up and said to Peter, 'You are one of them for sure! Why, your accent gives you away'. Then he started calling down curses on himself and swearing, 'I do not know the man'. At that moment the cock crew, and Peter remembered what Jesus had said, 'Before the cock crows you will have disowned me three times'. (Matt. 26:69–75)

Peter was placed in a situation of fear and he reacted as a frightened man. His faith was being tested in the harsh climate of the cold blast of hatred away from the hothouse atmosphere of the company of like-minded apostles. It is more rewarding to be a Christian when the dice are loaded against you. Peter was put to the test and failed miserably a few hours after his proud boast that 'though all lose faith in you, I will *never* lose faith'. Fear distracted him from Christ and he fell. He forgot who he was and betrayed his own faith which alone among the apostles had led him to follow Jesus into the courtyard of the high priest. He was spiritually close to his Master but his enemies were physically nearer. It was a desperate situation from which to extricate himself and so he denied that he even knew Jesus. How are the mighty fallen! The Vicar of Christ is driven into cursing and swearing by an illiterate serving-girl. I have never worried too much about the private failings of popes when I remember Peter!

20

Our strength will always remain our weakness when it leads to pride. How often in our lives do we come across people whom we considered paragons of perfection only to see them fall by the wayside. How silly it is to condemn them when we know, 'there but for the grace of God go I'. The Jewish blood still courses through our veins and the Pharisees still live on in us. For Peter the moment of truth came when his faith was put to the test and fear won. How would we react in a similar situation? We just do not know so it is not, nor ever should be, our place to condemn.

We cannot stand in judgement on anyone else's faith:

If a person's faith is not strong enough, welcome him all the same without starting an argument. People range from those who believe they may eat any sort of meat to those whose faith is so weak they dare not eat anything except vegetables. Meat-eaters must not despise the scrupulous. On the other hand, the scrupulous must not condemn those who feel free to eat anything they choose, since God has welcomed them. It is not for you to condemn someone else's servant: whether he stands or falls it is his own master's business; he will stand, you may be sure, because the Lord has power to make him stand. If one man keeps certain days as holier than others, and another considers all days to be equally holy, each must be left free to hold his own opinion. The one who observes special days does so in honour of the Lord. The one who eats meat does so also in honour of the Lord, since he gives thanks to God; but then the man who abstains does that too in honour of the Lord, and so he also gives God thanks. The life and death of each of us has its influence on others; if we live, we live for the Lord; and if we die, we die for the Lord, so that alive or dead we belong to the Lord. This explains why Christ both died and came to life, it was so that he might be Lord both of the dead and of the living. This is also why *you should never pass judgement on a brother or treat him with contempt*, as some of you have done. We shall all have to stand before the judgement seat of God; as scripture says: By my life – it is the Lord who speaks – every knee shall bend before me, and every tongue shall praise God. *It is to God, therefore, that each of us must give an account of himself.* Far from passing judgment on each other, therefore, you should make up your mind never to be the cause of your brother tripping or falling. (Rom. 14:1–12)

We avoid moralising about others since we know there is so much weakness in ourselves. Each of us has to live by the light of his own faith. The Christian who sees himself as holier than his neighbour is self-righteous. Only God sees our heart. In the same way the Church of Christ is always the first to acknowledge her own blemishes for which she repents. Self-defence is the attitude of the fearful and the churches which are quick to condemn others or see themselves as the only upholder of faith in God seem out of sympathy with the gospel.

Jesus understood the conflict inside Peter. He had been through it all before himself, especially in Gethsemane and knew the terrible toll that fear exacts from its victims. After his resurrection when he meets Peter again there is no word of reproach on his lips. He simply asks Peter the question:

'Simon, son of John, do you love me more than these others do?' He answered, 'Yes Lord, you know I love you'. Jesus said to him, 'Feed my lambs'. A second time he said to him, 'Simon, son of John, do you love me?' He replied, 'Yes, Lord, you know I love you'. Jesus said to him, 'Look after my sheep'. Then he said to him a third time, *'Simon, son of John, do you love me?'*

Peter was upset that he asked him a third time, 'Do you love me?' and said, *Lord, you know everything; you know I love you*'. Jesus said to him, 'Feed my sheep'. (John 21:15–17)

Jesus did indeed know everything; the triple denial and Peter weeping bitterly over what had been done. Love, in tears of sorrow, washes out our faults once we acknowledge them. When we look back on the times we have failed to speak out against those things which are in open conflict with our faith, instead of being remorseful we should concentrate on the love of Jesus which sees through and beyond our weakness. We may fail the Lord but we acknowledge our failure only because we love him and we know that he forgives us. We trust in his mercy rather than our own weakness.

There are situations all around the world when in the midst of the most frightening tortures men of faith dare to speak the unwelcome truth of the gospel. They stand up to be counted and for their faith suffer imprisonment and worse. On the other hand Christians, who should have spoken out, have remained silent because the preservation of their own image was their main motivating factor. Fear compromises faith.

No Christian denomination has the monopoly of those who stand up and are counted in the name of Christ. In Africa and South America today many denominations give brave witness to the Christian faith and we praise the Lord for them. The Spirit of God breathes where he wills today and it is our task to read the signs of the times. Jesus acknowledged the faith of the centurion and warned the Jews:

I tell you solemnly, nowhere in Israel have I found faith like this. And I tell you that many will come from the east and the west to take their places with Abraham and Isaac and Jacob at the feast in the kingdom of heaven; but the subjects of the kingdom will be turned out into the dark, where there will be weeping and grinding of teeth. (Matt. 8:10–12)

I have often wondered why so few Jews who were such a religious people failed to recognise Jesus as the Christ. I think the fault lies in the fact that they were so full of religion that they were lacking in faith. Their faith in Jesus as the Messiah was obscured by their preoccupation with religious observances which permeated every aspect of their lives. Religious bigotry arises when we are so biased in favour of our own sect or denomination that we are unable to see anything of value in other people's faith. I know many Protestants who will have nothing to do with me precisely because I am a 'Roman priest' about whom they choose to believe the most frightening stories. The same is also true of many Roman Catholics in their attitude to Protestants. The first time I spoke to a gathering of Methodists I was questioned by a very dour pillar of his Church as to why I did not join in the opening hymn. I asked him what he meant and he replied: 'You Romans have a reason for everything and I noticed you did not sing the hymn. Was there anything theological behind your silence? Why didn't you join us in praising the Lord?' 'Because', I replied, 'no one thought of giving me a hymn book and I did not know the words or the tune.' He did not seem to believe me and sat there for the rest of the meeting looking doubtful and fearful of the Roman invasion! However, these days are now over for enlightened Christians even though the old prejudices still exist once we dig beneath the surface. We should be all praising the Lord together in the name of Jesus for the wonderful faith which in his Spirit he has given to us. The healing of the Spirit is needed by all of us today to heal our hearts and minds so that we love one another as Christians should. We need to seek reconciliation with our brother first before we approach God's altar.

24

The tragedy with the Jews in their attitude to Jesus was:

Though they had been present when he gave so many signs, they did not believe in him; this was to fulfil the words of the prophet Isaiah: Lord, who could believe what we have heard said and to whom has the power of the Lord been revealed? Indeed, they were unable to believe because, as Isaiah says again: He has blinded their eyes, he has hardened their heart, for fear they should see with their eyes and understand with their heart, and turn to me for healing. Isaiah said this when he saw his glory, and his words referred to Jesus. *And yet there were many who did believe in him, even among the leading men, but they did not admit it, through fear of the Pharisees and fear of being expelled from the synagogue: they put honour from men before the honour that comes from God.* (John 12:37–43)

Like the Jews we also fear what our denominations will think of us when we sail too close to the ecumenical wind. We soon forget that as Christians we are called to be reconcilers. A staunch priest warned me years ago, after he heard me preach in an Anglican church which he reluctantly attended because he was asked to by his bishop, 'that I was becoming like one of them'. I was a threat to him without meaning to be. When I questioned him whether or not my preaching was orthodox he replied quite sincerely, 'You were alright but we are better living apart and you are trying to make us all one'! If that were my only fault then I should have cause to rejoice. Ecumenism is a threat when we are fearful that it will make us change our ways.

We lay perhaps too much emphasis on religion and not enough on faith. Before we condemn the Pharisees for their blindness it would be a good exercise to have a look at ourselves. When we tend to look over our shoulder too anxiously in the direction of our church leaders in order to gauge their reaction to everything we do, we may well fall into the trap of seeking religious approval to such an extent that we never show initiative or question anything. We cannot blame them if we choose to bury conscience beneath conformity or blind acquiescence. Each of us has to examine our own conscience before God and make our decision in faith and love. In this way we will seek what is pleasing to the Lord, and so help each other to find truth.

God calls each one of us by name. The most precious thing we possess is our freedom: without it we would not be human. We must never surrender it to anyone and when we act in conformity without thinking for ourselves then we are no better than robots. Christianity is all about the freedom which is given by the Spirit to those who confess that Jesus is Lord. Peter in the courtyard and the Jews, who believed in Jesus but did not follow him, forgot to be themselves. Fear robbed them of their individuality and ability to decide which course of action they would follow. They became 'mesmerised rabbits' and in doing so betrayed their vocation: Peter swore that he did not even know Jesus and the 'believing' Jews remained Jews.

Are we afraid to be different? afraid to be people of faith who live for God alone? If we are not afraid to stand up and be counted then the world will take notice of our faith which has helped us to dare to be different. The world needs us as leaven since it wants to believe but is afraid of the consequences. We can help to change all that if we believe that, through our faith, we have something to offer people who have got their priorities wrong. The Christian Churches ideally encourage us to have minds of our own but, if they too fall into the trap of excessive conformism, then they are no better than the secular systems of which they are supposed to be a contradiction. Churches rule by love; systems by fear.

Christians are not meant to be mediocre people who play for safety. We have a built-in mechanism called conscience which can make heroes not cowards of us all if we listen to its voice. Conscience is of paramount importance for the Christian and we give it pride of place in our lives. We believe that where human authorities are wrong we are able to appeal to a higher authority; the appeal to conscience is an appeal to God. We refuse to be carried along by the tide of popular opinion or majority consensus. Hitler asked the German people for their freedom for ten years and in return promised them a thousand years of world domination. Is it not strange that there were so relatively few who spoke up against him? 'What the majority wants is right' is the most pernicious philosophy which poisons our life-stream so that Christians are rightly suspicious of unanimous agreement in everything. If we are afraid to differ among ourselves as Christians on real issues then we have already imitated the world's standards. We can afford to criticize when we have put our own house in order. Unity is best expressed in diversity when we have our minds and wills fixed on the Lord. Uniformity is the pitfall of the compromiser with the easy answer.

Freedom of conscience presents each one of us with a challenge which helps us to mature as Christians. We cannot escape the personal agony of choice and the risk of failure. Conscience is our crisis and growth point. We will look for help in shouldering this responsibility from the Church communities and their leaders, but ultimately the choice rests between God and each individual. Jesus had his crisis points and we have ours. In the depths of our personality we dialogue with God but our ability to 'hear' him depends on our openness and sensitivity to him. Because we are damaged people 'we hear what we like'; nevertheless it is never a mistake to follow one's conscience. The alternative is blind, unthinking obedience to an external authority in whose judgement in this particular instance we do not believe. I dealt with the problems of 'authority and conscience' in my book *Seeking His Peace*. We cannot abdicate our human responsibility before God because that would mean denying that which is most deeply human in us. The Churches today need to teach in season and out of season our personal inviolability and inherent dignity as individuals. They should keep the person of Jesus constantly before us. When other systems tie us down with petty laws which restrict life, the Church allows us to enjoy its vision of our freedom as God's children.

The Jews who believed in Jesus but did not follow him 'loved the praise of men more than the praise of God'. It is hard to stand up and be counted especially if you find yourself like a voice crying in the wilderness. If we are to become people of conviction then we have to follow the call of the Spirit. It is not easy to reject expediency and social approval in our world which demands uniformity. We are afraid also to speak out clearly in love about those things in which we feel that as Churches we have strayed from the gospel message. We are not being disloyal to our Churches but dare to criticize only because we love them. In fact the extreme disloyalty would be to remain silent and give consent by collusion. We are critical of no one more than ourselves but we believe that there come times to speak out whatever the consequences to ourselves. Of course, we are troubled by the fear that we may be wrong and thus we bear the responsibility of leading others astray. Those who differ from us are following their own insights and vision which we respect as we all strive to be open to the Spirit. Jesus warns us:

Be on your guard: they will hand you over to sanhedrins; you will be beaten in synagogues; and *you will stand before governors and kings for my sake, to bear witness before them*, since the Good News must first be proclaimed to all the nations. And when they lead you away and hand you over, do not worry beforehand about what to say; no, say whatever is given to you when the time comes, because it is not you who will be speaking: it will be the Holy Spirit. Brother will betray brother to death, and father his child; children will rise against their parents and have them put to death. You will be hated by all men on account of my name; but the man who stands firm to the end will be saved. (Mark 13:9–13)

The so-called 'loyal' person is often seeking human approval and he already has his reward as a member of a chorus. Human approval is an alluring siren that attracts us to the calm shallows of safety on the shore on which we may be permanently beached. However, it is a dangerous and exciting voyage when we turn our faces to the wind. We are not meant to live as faceless people as the world would have us believe. 'Small is beautiful', and the individual person is God's gift to our universe. When we lose sight of the individual, then we are on the way to manipulation and the computer processing of human fodder which is needed only to keep the system going. Is this what life is all about?

We were born to live and grow in human society where we could be ourselves. We are not to be afraid of 'dialogue', speaking deep to deep concerning those things which we hold dear. The Church will grow as we grow within it when we are not a threat to it or vice versa. The greatest danger is that we will settle for an 'uneasy truce' in which we all play the game of loving each other without really meaning it. We will put on our masks for the outside world and avoid the unforgivable sin of letting the side down. We will become 'iron lung' people who cannot live without being accepted instead of coming fully alive in open dialogue with those who sincerely differ from us. If we are afraid to hurt each other it is surely because we do not believe in the other person's love. We play down our mutual respect until eventually it evaporates leaving nothing behind but the bitter salt of experience. If dialogue is a threat to any of us, perhaps it is because we do not want to hear the truth. We will have become a blocked artery in the blood stream of Christ's body causing paralysis of movement to any limb further down the system. The sight of a person suffering from the after-effects of a stroke always moves me. It is that image which I get whenever I encounter people who should be the Christian leaven of society, but are in fact a hindrance to the gospel without ever being aware of it. While it is regretted that their minds and hearts are closed, it is quite scandalous that they should inhibit others from living a full Christian life. Jealousy is the great inhibitor and surely I do not need to spell out the havoc that it causes in the lives of many Christians.

We seek the honour of men far too much. Human flattery is the trap door through which our spirituality disappears. We will not be listened to in society if we are too preoccupied in making the right noises or always banging the drum in favour of our own particular causes. When we appear to bolster up a secular society which is manifestly corrupt then our identification with Jesus is blurred. Church leaders spoke up against Hitler but too many engaged in a silence which gave consent. The Jews are rightly angry at our failure to expose the horror of the concentration camps. We may claim that we did not know but is this being strictly honest? Bonhoeffer speaks eloquently from the grave but he should have had more company. We are not to make friends of mammon; and the world sees behind the facade if we do. Consequently many sincere people opt out of belonging to any church, because they look upon the Churches as powerful organizations. It is true that we need to survive to preach the gospel but at what price to our Christian ideals? The Churches are thriving spiritually in the world whenever they oppose injustice and are persecuted because they dare to speak out in the name of oppressed peoples and nations; where they are politically powerful and seem to be thriving, they will die because they have betrayed themselves and the gospel of Jesus. God will sort them out at harvest time.

The world is beginning to show more concern for human rights in contemporary society and we are justifiably proud of the initiatives taken by Christian individuals and communities. They are daring to speak out and suffering torture in the process. They will be remembered in glory in some future time. We too can see myriad forms of injustice all round us in our local situation if only we are sensitive enough to appreciate them. The cry for 'human rights' finds an echo in all our hearts. The gospel of Christ reminds us that we are to love our neighbour and so risk involvement in our struggle for justice and peace for everyone. It is an ideal which, though we will never realize, we keep always before us. It is on these matters as well as doctrines of faith that we should stand up and be counted.

Martin Luther King suggests that in the parable of the Good Samaritan the priest and the Levite were afraid to stop and assist the wounded traveller in case they too should be attacked. They questioned: 'If I stop to help this man, what will happen to *me*?' The Samaritan, however, reversed the question: 'If I do not stop to help this man what will happen to *him*?' We too often ask the question: 'What will happen to me if I take a stand on an issue: what will happen to my job, my security, my future?' The people of real Christian conviction always reverse the question in their concern for others. 'What will happen to others if I don't make a stand?' Christians seek God's will above everything else so that their faith in him will overcome their fears about their life and future. They are not over-concerned with human esteem.

There are so many problems confronting us today that sometimes we do not know where to begin to stand up and be counted. Yet it is when everything seems hopeless that the Christian begins to hope. He starts where others would long before have thrown in the towel. We are called to a new hope in the Risen Lord. It is his victory on the cross which brings us new life and he alone will teach us his ways. We cannot put the world right, but we can change our own environment by allowing ourselves to be renewed daily. We will not know all the answers or even all the questions but those we ask will be the right ones. Of course failure will come our way and there will be times when we will be lowered into the well of loneliness, but we will never be alone. The Lord asks us too 'Do you love me?' and we reply: 'Lord, you know everything: you know I love you.' It is the love of Christ which is the driving force in our life. His spirit gives us the courage to face up to ourselves and every situation which we will encounter in the future. Paul writing to the Corinthians puts it in a dramatic way which is at once our challenge and support:

We are only the earthenware jars that hold this treasure, to make it clear that such an overwhelming power comes from God and not from us. We are in difficulties on all sides, but never cornered; we see no answer to our problems, but never despair; we have been persecuted, but never deserted; knocked down, but never killed; always, wherever we may be, we carry with us in our body the death of Jesus, so that the life of Jesus, too, may always be seen in our body. Indeed, while we are still alive, we are consigned to our death every day, for the sake of Jesus, so that in our mortal flesh the life of Jesus, too, may be openly shown. So death is at work in us, but life in you.

That is why there is no weakening on our part, and instead, though this outer man of ours may be falling into decay, the inner man is renewed day by day. Yes, the troubles which are soon over, though they weigh little, train us for the carrying of a weight of eternal glory which is out of all proportion to them. And so we have no eyes for things that are visible, but only for things that are invisible; for visible things last only for a time, and the invisible things are eternal. (2. Cor. 4:7–12, 16–18)

By his life-style Jesus shows us that a Christian does not conform to the standards of the world. We cannot court the world's popularity if we want to remain Christians. Paul exhorts us:

Do not model yourselves on the behaviour of the world around you, but let your behaviour change, modelled by your new mind. This is the only way to discover the will of God and know what is good, what it is that God wants, what is the perfect thing to do. (Rom. 12:2)

Our faith will conquer the world when as people of conviction we seek God's will for us above everything else. Solzhenitsyn warns us in the West against the 'triumphs of mediocrity' because of our decline in courage. He chides us for our 'intoxication with habitual extreme safety and well-being so that we are devoted to the letter of the law'. 'We have lost our willpower and so we turned our backs on the Spirit', he continues, 'and embraced all that is material with excessive zeal.'

True, we are afraid to stand up against the mainstream of opinion within the world but this is due to lack of faith and conviction on our part. If we were really convinced of the truth of our message, then we would proclaim it at whatever the cost to ourselves. 'Worldly' standards in the worst sense of the word have penetrated our thinking and life-style. Christians are too often indistinguishable from those who would never lay claim to having any sort of viable faith. It is not so much that we are not aware of the value of our faith for which, like

Peter, we would confess that we were prepared to lay down our lives, but rather that we are afraid to be different from those around us. We model ourselves on totally secular standards even within our Churches and the world is deprived of our witness.

The Soviet Jews who have been harshly sentenced for daring to monitor the Helsinki agreement have something of value to say to us about standing up for our beliefs. The Soviet government calls them 'dissidents': I call them witnesses. The word witness means martyrdom and by it we witness to the power of the Spirit of Truth within us. Power even in the Churches will always seek to crush the individual who threatens it because power is basically an evil and corrupting force. It rules by fear and innuendo rather than direct punishment which is its last resort. It then seeks in self-justification to make the crime fit the punishment. Fearless witness is necessary to counterbalance the evils of power:

If the world hates you,
remember that it hated me before you.
If you belonged to the world,
the world would love you as its own;
but because you do not belong to the world,
because my choice withdrew you from the world,
therefore the world hates you.
Remember the words I said to you:
A servant is not greater than his master.
If they persecuted me,
they will persecute you too;

If I had not performed such works among them
as no one else has ever done,
they would be blameless;
but as it is, they have seen all this,
and still they hate both me and my Father.
But all this was only to fulfil the words written in their
Law:

They hated me for no reason.
When the Advocate comes,
whom I shall send to you from the Father,
the Spirit of Truth who issues from the Father,
he will be my witness.
And you too will be witnesses,
because you have been with me from the outset.

I have told you all this
so that your faith may not be shaken.
They will expel you from the synagogues,
and indeed the hour is coming
when anyone who kills you will think he is doing a
holy duty for God.
They will do these things
because they have never known either the Father or
myself.
But I have told you all this,
so that when the time for it comes
you may remember that I told you. (John 15: 18–20;
25–7; 16:4)

The gospel of Jesus is lived out in each one of us who
uses it as a way of life. Our Master knew what it was to
face up to power, both religious and secular, and he was
crucified for his belief. His life was a contradiction of
everything that the Jews of the time seemed to want.
They were not prepared to accept and understand the
'dreamer' who stood in their midst. When the going is
easiest for us, then we can be sure that somewhere along
the line we have compromised ourselves. This can happen too easily to a Christian when his faith is reduced to
religious ritual so that the clear waters of truth have
become stagnant. The Christian life is an ongoing process in dialogue with the world which is forever asking us
new questions. If we listen not only to it but also to the
Holy Spirit, we will begin to rediscover what the Lord is

asking of us. We are the world's heart-transplant which the world constantly seeks to reject yet without which it would not really live. We are witnesses of a higher order. The true power of the Church has been its courage to proclaim the message of Jesus in the face of overwhelming odds. In every age we have our witnesses to the power of the gospel and every country's faith is watered by the blood of martyrs.

The Christian life is indeed a battle with the forces of evil. Paul compares us to soldiers in God's army:

> Finally, grow strong in the Lord, with the strength of his power. Put God's armour on so as to be able to resist the devil's tactics. For it is not against human enemies that we have to struggle, but against the Sovereignties and the Powers who originate the darkness in this world, the spiritual army of evil in the heavens. That is why *you must rely on God's armour, or you will not be able to put up any resistance when the worst happens, or have enough resources to hold your ground.* So stand your ground, with truth buckled round your waist, and integrity for a breastplate, wearing for shoes on your feet the eagerness to spread the gospel of peace and always carrying the shield of faith so that you can use it to put out the burning arrows of the evil one. And then you must accept salvation from God to be your helmet and receive the word of God from the Spirit to use as a sword. (Ephesians 6:10–17)

We dare not underestimate the power of the devil but neither should we forget that God is on our side. Victory is ours since Jesus has already conquered the world. It will never be easy to look beyond the dark clouds of uncertainty which tend to limit our vision, but we have to keep on trying to be true to the gospel entrusted to us. We are not afraid to face up to the weaknesses in ourselves since, though we are all damaged by sin, the message is greater than the messenger. Like Peter on occasions we will seek the easy way out but we must keep on trying. We will not be inhibited by the fact that our message is unpopular to the majority of our listeners even within our own denomination or group.

There are prophets in all the Christian communities not only for the world but for the communities themselves. A prophet in the twentieth century is Pope John XXIII who spoke not only to Catholics and to all Christians but to the world. The world may not have listened but the fault was not his. Thoreau says: 'If a man does not keep pace with his companions perhaps it is because he hears a different drummer. Let him step to the music which he hears however different and far away.'

We hear God's call and we respond each in his own way. If others do not respond because they choose to bury conscience then that is their responsibility. What matters to us is that we respond and witness to the Risen Lord, as Peter did so courageously in the First Pentecost and to which the believing Jews responded. 'They were convinced by his arguments, and they accepted what he said and were baptised. That very day about three thousand were added to their number.' (Acts 2:41). The world, like the Jews, may not have listened in the past but it may well listen now if, when we receive the Spirit, like Peter we cast aside our fears to stand up and be counted. We will come alive knowing that we have not betrayed ourselves, nor denied our faith:

Do not be afraid of them therefore. For everything that is now covered will be uncovered, and everything now hidden will be made clear. What I say to you in the dark, tell in the daylight; what you hear in whispers, proclaim from the housetops. Do not be afraid of those who kill the body but cannot kill the soul; fear him rather who can destroy both body and soul in hell. Can you not buy two sparrows for a penny? And yet

37

not one falls to the ground without your Father knowing. Why, every hair on your head has been counted. So there is no need to be afraid; you are worth more than hundreds of sparrows. So if anyone declares himself for me in the presence of men, I will declare myself for him in the presence of my Father in heaven. But the one who disowns me in the presence of men, I will disown in the presence of my Father in heaven. (Matt. 10:26–33)

3. Why is there fear in the Church?

There has always been fear in the Church and there always will be. Jesus knew fear in himself since it is part and parcel of our damaged human nature and surely we are not greater than he. We inherited fear from the fall of man and it will be our companion to the end of time. If Jesus was not immune, then how can we ever begin to claim that fear has nothing to do with our lives as Christians? The very concept of fear in the Church causes indignation to many self-righteous Christians who presume that the Church is above fear. This is very dangerous thinking and affords a perfect breeding ground for the spread of the disease. The Church will not grow as it should unless and until we admit that we are still prone to fear and that it is one of our greatest enemies. C. S. Lewis reminds us in the *Screwtape Letters* that the devil has a field day among those who do not believe that he exists.

Fear among us as Christians is very real and the greatest disservice we could do to the Church is to pretend that we live on such an exalted plane that fear has no terrors for us. It exists in the Church at all levels because the Church is composed of people who despite their Christian calling and divine assistance are still human and damaged. It takes courageous and holy people to acknowledge that they are afraid. The most attractive

39

element in the Church, especially in recent times, has been its readiness to confess its faults and fears. Pope John XXIII endeared himself to the whole world when he asked forgiveness for any sins his Church had committed against fellow Christians. He was not afraid to admit that we are not all saints all the time; he shed the Pharisee's robe of self-righteousness where to acknowledge fear was a sign of weakness. The fearful person suppresses fear and will go to extreme lengths to demonstrate his power and strength both to himself and to others. Fear spawns power with its attendant evils. The Church that does not see fear as a threat to itself uses fear to threaten others and becomes a power machine.

We have to come face to face with the fears within ourselves which hinder us from growing to maturity as full persons. We do this at a human level in order to fight fear so that it may lose its power over us. The Christian faith helps us to become fully human so that thus we strip fear of its terror, when we see it for what it is. We are afraid as Christians not because of our faith but because of our lack of it. Even though we believe as Christians that God is a loving Father who will not allow us to be tempted and threatened more than we are able to sustain and conquer, yet we are still afraid because we do not trust him enough and in this lies the constant battle between faith and fear. Truth is the detergent which disperses the oil slick of fear.

We are encouraged in the gospels to follow the example of Jesus and thus commit ourselves in trust to God, our Father, who loves us more than we love ourselves. We need to reassure ourselves time and time again of this love if we are not to slip back again into the shadows of fear. As Christians we are called to walk in the light of the resurrection: 'Wake up from your sleep, rise from the dead, and Christ will shine on you' (Eph. 5:14). Jesus has conquered sin, death, and the world. The less fearful we are the more we will be united with the victorious Lord and the more ready the whole Church will be through us to fulfil its mission. My faith which diminishes fear increases the effective presence of the Church in the world; my fear diminishes it. We all bring a plus or minus of faith to the Church. Faith and fear fill our blood stream like red and white corpuscles; faith for red and fear for white. Fear makes us blanch or go white; faith fills us with the sanguine hope of victory. We are aglow with faith in the Lord Jesus and allow his life to course through our veins. We have to beware of spiritual leukaemia which is a disease caused by an excess of fear.

Jesus overcame his own personal fear in Gethsemane and fear, like faith, is very personal. When I say that the Church is full of fear I am only saying that I am fearful and I am part of the Church. I know how difficult it is to conquer fear in myself and there are times when I would rather live much more tranquilly; but life is not like that and God has chosen that my priesthood has fitted into twenty-five years of momentous development in the history of the Church. There is something deep within me which keeps me going. We are challenged on all sides today as Christians, from within and without, so that faith and fear have come out into the open to engage in a furious battle.

I have never known more fear and faith around me since Pope John XXIII called the Second Vatican Council. We live in an exciting time for the Church. Many people in high places are so afraid of the future that they would like to go back to the status quo *ante* and so forget the nightmare of the Council. The Church, they say, must withdraw from the world in order to consolidate. Their faith has been shaken by all the disturbances over the past sixteen years and they want to preserve what they can. They have a lot of reason on their side and should not be dismissed out of hand.

On the other side there are visionaries of faith whose

horizons would require the sacrifices of the apostles in the Early Church so that like them we should be ready to sell all to follow Jesus. They are radical gospel Christians and are prepared to let the institutional Church die whatever the consequences. In the middle are people who are a varied mixture of faith and fear vacillating from one side to the other. They want the changes in the Church to be more gradual yet want the Church to grow.

It is to them all that the risen Jesus says 'Peace be with you'. In a state of alarm and fright after his passion and death the apostles thought they were seeing a ghost when the risen Jesus appeared to them but he said: '"Why are you so agitated, and why are these doubts rising in your hearts? Look at my hands and feet; yes, it is I indeed. Touch me and see for yourselves; a ghost has no flesh and bones as you see I have." And as he said this he showed them his hands and feet. Their joy was so great that they still could not believe it, and they stood there dumb-founded' (Luke 24:37–41).

We find it extremely difficult to accept as a fact of our daily lives that the Risen Lord is with us in all our trials and tribulations. Growth in the Church of tomorrow depends on the measure of our faith today. The great gift that we can give to our Church is the belief that every-thing that is happening now, whether we like it or not, is ultimately for the good of the Church. I believe the Kingdom of God is winning and in the process Jesus overcomes our fears and breaks through structures, which we thought were indispensable, as easily as he emerged from the tomb. The authorities put soldiers on guard over it, as well as sealing it with a huge stone, but Jesus was not deterred by these minor obstacles. He loves people absolutely and structures only if they help people. The risen Jesus rises fresh every morning to give us new hope to go on believing in him and his Church. He is our Easter joy who tells us, 'Peace be with you'.

The apostles during the public ministry of Jesus had

their bad as well as their good days. Often when things would seem to augur well, events would soon change and a crisis would develop:

> With the coming of evening that same day, he said to them, 'Let us cross over to the other side'. And leaving the crowd behind they took him, just as he was, in the boat; and there were other boats with him. Then it began to blow a gale and the waves were breaking into the boat so that it was almost swamped. But he was in the stern, his head on the cushion, asleep. *They woke him and said to him, 'Master, do you not care? We are going down!'* And he woke up and rebuked the wind and said to the sea, 'Quiet now! Be calm!' And the wind dropped, and all was calm again. *Then he said to them, 'Why are you so frightened? How is it that you have no faith?'* They were filled with awe and said to one another, 'Who can this be? Even the wind and the sea obey him.' (Mark 4:35–41)

Jesus often seems to be asleep in his Church and we wonder if he really cares at all. It is a great strength of the Church that she has survived self-inflicted wounds of every kind. These can recur, and it would be sheer folly to consider ourselves more enlightened than previous generations. Even if the Church did renege for a time on all the promises of faith and vision of the council or the radicals leave us with little visible structures, our individual faith would keep it going until a more favourable time when the Spirit would once again blow it in the right direction. It is faith that has kept the Barque of Peter afloat and it is faith that will keep its sails open to the breath of the Spirit. The Church is still the Body of Christ come what may.

Some people hold that the Church has been weakened over the past decade and its influence is decreasing. If this were true, which I doubt, then all will be well if Jesus

43

is still with it. Why are we afraid for the Church? He has given his promise and he will keep it, and now it is up to us to keep faith with him. We, like the apostles, are frightened, but our fears concern ourselves in the final analysis and not the Church; 'Master, do you not care? We are going down.'

We want our kind of Church to remain and believe that ours is the only solution to its problems. Such arrogance is born from dangerous self-conceit and not from the reserves of faith. We can become so religiously orientated in our own set ways as to render ourselves bereft of belief that it is basically Christ's Church through which God's kingdom comes and not our own personal judgements. We are all the people of God from pope to the smallest child and we need to listen to each other in love. This is the dialogue which is so necessary to the Church today. When we talk to each other from positions of strength, then there is little hope of dialogue, but when we approach each other as gifts and not as threats, then we will be imitating the humility and openness of the Lord. We are not to worry about who is the greatest or whose ideas will prevail. Christ is the peace between us.

We will disagree over many things in the Church but we will remain a loving family, provided we are prepared to listen and are not victims of the dreadful disease called 'instant wisdom'. If we only want the Church to go in the direction we want then we become more and more polarized, so that we are either frightened by all the changes happening in our time or dismayed that the Church is moving too slowly. We cannot have it all our own way if we want it to be Christ's way. He says to us, 'Why are you frightened? How is it that you have no faith?'

Faith motivated by love never threatens anyone except ourselves when it makes us move out of entrenched and comfortable positions. We are often too secure in the Church – as to be over-anxious about our own position or else we want change irrespective of what people feel.

Sometimes we are prepared to let others fight it out because we are too apathetic and just want to let the dust settle. Apathy is the inertia born of spiritual, physical and mental laziness. The Church is more apathetic than fearful and this is the real tragedy of our age. Our need today is for a lively faith which will blow through the becalmed world of our time as a challenge and inspiration. We must face up to crises and not pretend that they do not exist. Together with Christ we overcome the problems confronting the Church today, confident in the knowledge that Christ is with us always to the ends of the earth and the end of time.

What are the basic problems confronting us today in the Church which make us fearful? Many people are afraid that the Church is losing its grip as regards its witness to the world because it is racked by internal dissension. On the one side there is a legitimate appeal to return to a more disciplined structured Church in which answers would be forthcoming on every conceivable subject; on the other there are those who hold that the claims of conscience cannot be ignored if we are to grow as mature Christians in a challenging world where the rights of individuals are being suppressed. It is a question of authority and conscience and there is no reason why it should not be resolved, if we all engage in true, open and honest dialogue. Once we allow fear to take over, then people are going to be hurt unnecessarily and the Church will suffer. We need to possess our souls in peace and listen to the Spirit as he shows us the way ahead.

It is only to be expected that changes in authority structures should by their nature introduce fear. The Christian is being asked today to think for himself, perhaps more than at any other period of history. True, he will still look to the Church's authority for direction and guidance, but religion is no longer the secure and comforting factor that it once was. We may not always relish the responsibility of deciding for ourselves or worse still we may become a law unto ourselves, so that anarchy abounds under the guise of an over-indulgence of private judgement. The Church and the individual should not be in conflict when all are motivated by deep human respect based on love. It is in the conflict of 'the one and the many' that fear appears, and to combat it we have to rely on faith in God and the Church of which we are all parts, each having a vital role to play:

> Just as a human body, though it is made up of many parts, though many, make one body, so it is with Christ. In the one Spirit we were all baptised, Jews as well as Greeks, slaves as well as citizens, and one Spirit was given to us all to drink. Nor is the body to be identified with any one of its many parts. If the foot were to say, 'I am not a hand and so I do not belong to the body', would that mean that it stopped being part of the body? If the ear were to say, 'I am not an eye, and so I do not belong to the body', would that mean that it was not a part of the body? If your whole body was just one eye, how would you hear anything? If it was just one ear, how would you smell anything? . . .
> *Now you together are Christ's body; but each of you is a different part of it.* (1 Cor. 12:12–17,27)

The crisis of authority is a crisis concerning the nature and function of the Church. Authority is essential to the Church, since we are a visible body of believers whose spiritual head is Christ and we are distinguishable by belief and conduct from those who are not Christians. What is the Church for and how can it best function as a witness to the world? The answers to these questions dictate the role of everyone from the Pope to the individual in the pew.

All authority today, whether religious or secular, is suspect. Our age has emphatically rejected the authoritarian use of power so that the monolithic ideal of authority is no longer acceptable. The dictatorship of the thirties made absolute obedience suspect and the rise of communism, together with the increasing social consciousness of Christians, have made us question privileged structures. Youth with its ideals, human rights, and other modern phenomena disclose not only our world's thinking but determine the Church's mission. Vatican II and Pope Paul VI's radical encyclical 'Populorum Progressio' have given a new cutting edge to the Church. Christians who are held up for our edification like Mother Teresa of Calcutta and Archbishop Helder Camara come not from the West but from the Third World. We live in a new age and the Church is *searching* for a new voice in which to articulate its message. That it is doing so should make us all grateful to the Spirit who is its guide, telling us that we must renew ourselves and look outwards to a world crying to us for leadership in matters concerning justice and peace. More than anything else today we are a 'searching Church'.

Vatican II marked a watershed in the development of our growing awareness of conscience. We go forward from the Council together in dialogue at once deep and trustful. A renewed Church will emerge strengthened in authority and individual conscience. If we do not believe this, then all the pain involved in the Church since 'Humanae Vitae' would seem to be in vain. The controversies of today are nothing compared to those which nearly split the Church at the Council of Jerusalem. Our faith in the Church as Christ's presence among us is being put to the test now and we must not be afraid. If we read the account of the Council of Jerusalem, Acts, Chapter 15 then we will realize that our controversy is a mere storm in a teacup. We remember how Jesus calmed the storm and rebuked the disciples: 'Why are you so frightened? How is it that you have no faith?' (Mark 4:40). What Jesus did once he will do again, once we turn to him and put aside our fear. The crisis in the Church seems to me not so much a question of authority and conscience but of faith. If we fail now then the whole world will suffer the loss of our united witness.

The relevant questions today concern participation in the life of the Church in which no one is a second-class citizen. Just as we are not developed as complete persons unless we allow our hidden selves to realize their full potential, so too in the Church I believe we are about to enter the age of the laity and thus the Church will become a more effective witness in the world. If the laity are encouraged generously to make their apostolic contribution then indeed the face of the earth will be renewed. We must take the principles of collegiality and subsidiarity to their logical conclusion. There is a danger of a greater dichotomy arising between the clergy and laity than exists at present. In recent years some judgements of the 'clerical Church' were questioned by the laity and it did not take kindly to a reversal of its role and fortune. In many cases I have found more wisdom from the laity than I have from the clergy precisely because they were giving me the fruits of their particular expertise. The clergy have their own insights to give and thus working more closely together we would all make a great team. Recently I was told by a Methodist minister that he resented prayer groups in his congregation because his people knew more about prayer than he did! He is not alone in this phobia about prayer groups, however much clergy may rationalize about them. Prayer groups which are motivated by the Spirit are not *per se* easily susceptible to clerical leadership.

We are not to be afraid of each other or to wield power over anyone but remain open to reconciliation with each other, and this means putting aside all those differences and prejudices which keep us apart. We must learn to love and respect each other more deeply than we have in the past by acknowledging the inherent dignity of each individual. The Church has emphasized laws too much in the past and so instilled fear rather than love. The real authority in our lives as Christians is to love as Jesus did. The lawgiver sees his life as a very complex pattern of virtues and vices in which the observance of the law holds pride of place. The Pharisees were guilty of the same mistake. The fulfilment of law for us and that which gives it meaning is love.

When we look at gospel authority we will see it as a mission from Christ to proclaim his reconciling gospel. That is the real authority which the Church has. She has no power except over sin and the forces of evil. When Church authority moves into the realm of any other kind of power, then it becomes the antithesis of that for which it was founded. The authority of the Church is to proclaim the gospel in its entirety and thus to protect it from myth, parody and distortion. The gospel means good news by which we are liberated from the servitude of meaningless laws and customs and the opening up to us of undreamed-of possibilities of life, achievement and happiness.

The authority of the Church is derivative; it comes from Christ. We must use it therefore as Christ would use it. When people see a clear disparity between our exercise of authority and Christ's they do not listen to our voice. Authoritarianism leads to a rejection of the institutional Churches. The strange phenomenon of our time is that, while interest in Jesus Christ has increased and while more people acknowledge that they are theists, fewer people confess allegiance to organized religion. If we look outside our own petty quarrels then we will see the world through the eyes of Jesus: 'And when he saw the crowds he felt sorry for them because they were harassed and dejected, like sheep without a shepherd. Then he said to his disciples: "The harvest is rich but the labourers are few, so ask the Lord of the harvest to send labourers to his harvest" ' (Matt. 9:36–7).

How can we reconcile the past few centuries of oligarchic rule with the sudden change in emphasis by Vatican II on individual conscience? How does this approach coincide with tradition? Father Yves Congar, I think, has the answer. He sees tradition as the continuity of being open to new conditions in the changing world. He hopes that through the changes today we will 'recover the deep aspirations of the Church at those times when she has been most purely herself, above all in the third, fourth and fifth centuries. The time of the martyrs first of all, and then of the great councils which gave the Church her dogmas, the essential structures of her canon law, her interior discipline and the form of her liturgy. The time of the fathers, of Basil, Chrysostom, Gregory of Nyssa, Gregory of Nazianza, Cyril of Alexandria, Augustine, Jerome, Ambrose, Hilary, Leo, all these great saints, these great geniuses'. The new Jerusalem is at our door perhaps while we remain locked inside bemoaning the fact that the Church is changing. All the controversy over the past decade will be well worth while since it is part of God's plan for our renewal and new life in the Church. We will recover the authentic *sensus fidelium* because we will have listened to and consulted the laity. Are we entering another Golden Age? It could be if you and I were more receptive to the Spirit.

Another fear confronting many Catholics and other Christians is, paradoxically, Christian unity. This is an enterprise which is full of pitfalls and dangers. The greatest danger of all, of course, is apathy – to bury our heads in the sand and do nothing at all. Not only are we in danger of being misunderstood but there is also a very real danger of diminishing doctrine rather than enriching it. In our desire to come together in corporate unity we may settle for the lowest common multiple in our traditions. Perhaps our emphasis on corporate unity has tended to overlook the unity of spirit in Christ, which is the only type worth having, since it is the basis of any other form of meaningful unity. If we are really united in Christ and remain open to the Spirit then corporate unity will follow.

We owe it to Christ to go forward together to make him better known and followed. The real goal, therefore, is Christian witness and only Christian unity in so far as it helps our witness to Christ. If we work together we may learn to grow together and thus establish a unity of witness and fellowship while still maintaining, at least for a time, our separate corporate bodies. Is this what God wants and is this the type of unity for which Christ prayed, 'that they all may be one'? We have become so damaged by history that we are forced to live with the consequences of our sins. We can remain true to our traditions and still be prepared to change. We need to pray to discover what God's will is for us in our broken Jerusalem.

We are divided among ourselves as Christians not only by doctrine but by different ways of life especially in the West. Christian unity presents very few problems in those parts of the world where people are not infected with our western prejudices. In the West the doctrinal issues are closely associated with a whole host of things only incidentally connected with doctrine, yet these 'incidentals' are so precious to many Catholics that they are not prepared to jettison them. This is especially true of converts, many of whom see ecumenism as a sell-out.

Religion has become a way of life and we have accustomed ourselves to living apart. To modify religion is to modify life and life changes slowly. Those who are over-addicted to a religious denomination are today's bigots who are 'anti' the others rather than 'pro' their own Church. They are proud of their differences, like the Pharisee who went up to the temple and spent so much of his time criticizing others, especially the publican, that he forgot to pray. I have met many bigots on all sides on the rocky road to Christian unity over the past twenty

51

years and bear the battle scars in my memory. It was not uncommon for me after my talk to other Christians to hear expressions of surprise that they had met a Catholic who was a Christian. Shades of Northern Ireland!

I remember one incident which stays with me very forcibly over the years and occurred in a parish where I was a curate. I had discovered a 'lapsed' Catholic, Tom, who was married outside the Catholic Church and there was no way in which I could regularize his marriage. Tom was not exactly gospel greedy and I never got far with him whenever I broached the subject of religion. His wife was staunchly Church of England and when he died she decided to have him buried in her church graveyard. For some strange reason she invited me to say 'prayers over him' but the local vicar was not very pleased. He allowed me to come only when he had finished his ritual and departed to his vicarage. A few days afterwards I was given a severe dressing down by authority for daring to bury a Catholic in Protestant soil! I do not think either side comes out of the story well when it even claims the soil as Catholic or Protestant! Please God those days are nearly gone.

It must be obvious to any of us who dare to call ourselves Christians that our distrust of each other, manifested in disunity, is a hindrance to Christ's mission to our world. Robert McAfee Brown, a Protestant theologian, writing on the Vatican Council, sums up my attitude: 'To ask the world to unite in a common unity is flabby advice when those making the request are not even able to unite among themselves.' The same theme was taken up by the bishops in the Second Vatican Council when they stated that: 'The division in Christendom is an open contradiction to the will of Christ and the world finds it scandalous. It is damaging to the whole cause of preaching the gospel to every creature.' Divisions among Christians in so far as they impede our witness to Christ are sinful if we deliberately perpetuate them or by omission fail to eradicate them.

No one is so foolish as to envisage that Christian unity is just round the corner. We cannot undo overnight the damage inflicted by centuries of living, thinking and praying apart. Dr Visser t'Hooft described our age as one in which we have to learn to live, work and grow together before we can take any far-reaching steps in actual reunion. These steps are being taken now by church leaders with their respective commissions which do invaluable work. I believe most strongly, however, that Christian unity will grow upwards from ordinary people who come together simply because they can see no reason for living apart. Fear of Christian unity tends to be a clerical hazard and the laity will shepherd us along sometimes protesting to the altar rails for the wedding of our Churches! It is time that the courtship got under way in those places where as yet we have only graduated to polite conversations at clergy fraternals.

The great change of attitude today among Christians of all Churches is to see other Christians in a positive light; to define them by what they possess rather than what they lack; to stress what unites rather than what divides; to encourage dialogue so that we see the other's point of view from his point of view. It is because of this latter aspect of dialogue that we must listen to the people. We are a searching Church. I have been involved in ecumenism at all levels, including five years as Consultor to the Secretariat for Christian Unity at the Vatican and six years on our National Ecumenical Commission, and I am convinced that the time has come to go back to our roots in ordinary people. What is the 'sensus fidelium' on Christian unity? If ever we superimpose corporate unity on the people we will be as guilty as those who today drag their feet.

Christian unity is God's gift to his people and we must not stand in the way. I realize that I am not saying anything deeply theological about ecumenism, since I prefer to deal with approaches and attitudes of ordinary people rather than commissions and committees. Top level commissions are necessary in affording initiatives and formalizing statements, but the main thrust for Christian unity will come from the people as they become more aware of where the Spirit is leading them. Both approaches are complementary but the 'listening to the people' has not been sufficiently emphasized or undertaken.

Why are Christians coming together now and not before? We were 'happy' in our separate Churches so why not leave everyone to his own Church? Has the Catholic Church changed its doctrine in recent years? Have we been wrong up to now, believing that we were the True Church? The Spirit of the Risen Lord is abroad in our world and he is blowing the Churches together for his own good purposes. Vatican II gave us a new way of looking at the Church which is in sharp contrast to that envisaged by the encyclical 'Mystici Corporis'. The Church of Christ is a 'mystery' and it 'subsists' in the Roman Catholic Church so that we as Catholics do belong to the True Church as indeed we always believed we did. However, the Roman Catholic Church does not exhaust the power of the Spirit in the Church of Christ. What this means as regards the various Churches has still to be explained more carefully and simply so that we all know exactly where we stand. In other words Catholics are Christians but not the only ones. It is to achieve full unity between the Churches that we are striving. How this will come about we do not know.

We have nothing to be afraid of because Jesus has promised that '. . . when the Spirit of truth comes he will lead you to the complete truth' (John 16:13). We are growing towards the truth in every age, since truth is a dynamic, growing gift of the Spirit in our lives as Christians. We should not claim so much to possess the truth as to be possessed by it. The more we empty ourselves of our arrogance, the more we will become truth-filled by the Spirit. That is not to say we were wrong in the past: it was right for that particular age, but we are pilgrims and the Spirit is leading us now to what is necessary to our belief today.

Instead of thinking along terms of 'big ecclesiastical mergers' we need to 'think small' in terms of the individual or the small group. If as Catholics we come to terms with our Protestant neighbour so that we both appreciate each other's differences, then Christian unity is being made that much easier. I have seen this issue clearly in terms of the individual as a result of my work for peace in Northern Ireland. If we all become better (not bigoted) Catholics and Protestants because of our inner conversion to Christ, we will become better Christians. It is our unity in Christ which is the essential unity for which we all pray. Christ is the way to unity and he is also the truth of unity, namely, that God is the Father of us all:

Consecrate them in the truth;
your word is truth.
As you sent me into the world,
I have sent them into the world,
and for their sake I consecrate myself
so that they too may be consecrated in truth.
I pray not only for these,
but for those also
who through their words will believe in me.
May they all be one.
Father, may they be one in us,
as you are in me and I in you,
so that the world may believe it was you who sent me.
I have given them the glory you gave to me,
that they may be one as we are one.
With me in them and you in me,
may they be so completely one

55

that the world will realise that it was you who sent me.
(John 17:17–23)

There is no need to be afraid of each other in the Church
if we are true Christians. The Spirit will guide us towards
loving acceptance of each other so that unity, like happiness, will come without our really planning for it. If we
witness together, we will grow together. I praise the Lord
for all my wonderful Christian brothers and sisters from
the different Churches who witness with me before an
increasingly sophisticated world. We need 'big-minded'
Christians today who trust one another with the God-
given gift of witnessing to the power of Christ. I have
been helped in myriad ways by my brethren in Christ. I
do not talk any more of 'separated' brethren, because we
cannot be separated if we are brothers and sisters in the
Lord.

I thank God for all he has given me in the Church
through my parents, family, friends and wonderful
Christian people whom I would never have known so
specially if I had not been a Christian myself. They have
given me hope in and for the Church: a hope that is
liberating and saving and gives us a courage knowing
that we are not alone. We do not know what tomorrow
will bring us as Catholics or to the other Christian
Churches, but great things will be done through us if we
turn our whole lives towards the Lord. The world may
not join our ranks but they will know we are Christians
by our love.

4. Are you afraid of change?

On my desk is a small card which says, 'Cheer up. Change is here to stay.' It is my way of letting people know that I am above all a person of hope and an optimist. I do not believe we have any other option as Christians. Pessimists are conservatives because they have no real vision of joy and adventure. They are fearful, suspicious people who cling to what they have. Change in any form in religious or secular spheres threatens them, because acceptance of the status quo is their ultimate definition of happiness based on security. They are apprehensive of change and find it disturbing in their lives. Their constant complaint is that nothing lasts and so they sing with heartfelt approval to God, 'O Thou (not you) Who changest not, abide with me'. Frightened people are basically afraid of venturing beyond the familiar so that religion becomes a surfeit of nostalgia. The pessimist is always remembering the 'good old days' and looks forward to the future only with apprehension. He can envisage no change for the better but only the worse.

The Christian optimist is one who attempts to live out a dream and insists that, since the world is changing for better or worse, then it can only be for the better through his intervention. He immerses himself in the world as part of a great adventure believing that the whole human, not merely Christian, society is being changed by Christ. The world and the Church are changing because they are interactive and Christ is the man for everyman. He sees the Holy Spirit inviting us to take a risk, telling us that the news is good while challenging us with its uncompromising message. It reminds us that we are pilgrims. The optimist gives flesh and blood to his vision and like Martin Luther King is considered one of society's gadflies. He burns bridges behind him as he ventures out into the unknown simply in the hope that the new land will unfold before his eyes over the next mountain top. His loneliness with few to share his vision makes him society's hairshirt and a joy to youth. He is usually one of the world's walking wounded and stead-fastly refuses to accept things as they are, because he still dreams of things as they might be. He is a rebel with peace in his heart who will resist compromise come what may.

The majority of people are apprehensive of change and find it disturbing in their lives. The more fixed they are in their ways and modes of thinking, the more difficult it is for them to accept even the smallest alteration to the status quo. They are even slower to accept changes in religious matters than they are in secular. Roman Catholics were turned upside down and inside out by the Second Vatican Council. The lives of millions of people were deeply disturbed and everything they held dear seemed to disappear overnight. The Church, although it has not changed fundamentally, nevertheless appears less certain of where it is going. An American visitor was given the privilege of an audience with Pope Paul VI and asked him where and what was the Church. The Pope replied: 'It is the mystery of Christ.' The American wrung his hands in disbelief: 'Gosh, Holy Father, for two thousand years it was us Catholics with you as the Head and now you tell us it is a mystery. Has it taken us two thousand years to find that out?'

It is more difficult now to be a Catholic than it was twenty years ago, since it is easier to reject Catholicism without incurring the sometimes abusive disapproval of those who remain within the fold. The word 'Judas' came all too easily in the past to the lips to describe a 'defector'. All that has now changed except in the minds and hearts of the 'old guard'. Charity has superseded loyalty as the cardinal virtue and Catholics today are given a vision of their Church which is more humble and authentic than at any time since the early centuries. The 'Second Pentecost' has arrived and the Spirit of Christ blows where it wills, even though to many it came not as a gentle breeze but as a hurricane lifting up their homes and carrying them out of sight. Vatican II left many spiritually homeless people of all shades of ecclesiastical hue in its wake and we have not had sufficient compassion for them nor understanding of their plight. The implementation of the Council's decrees in this country, especially as regards liturgical changes, was in the opinion of many people pastorally insensitive and autocratically imposed. The claim that it was necessary to enforce the liturgical changes overnight, in order to make them catch on everywhere, is about as naive as trying to paint the Mona Lisa with a farmyard brush because it is quicker.

To many traditionalists the Catholic Church had changed overnight and had undergone a measure of secularization. It was less urgent, not only in its demands for membership, but in its enforcement of its laws, especially in the realm of sex; 'Humanae Vitae' is dead through non-observance. It is insecure, they say, in a world which needs the strength of its unchangeable message. They bemoan the fact that it seems to have diminished itself by a form of ecclesiastical 'hara kiri' so that now it is in disarray. For them there is a new kind of prophet like Archbishop Lefebvre emerging who recalls our past heritage and warns us of the dangers of flirting with the world.

Catholics today, they say, are made to feel insecure and guilty of all the sins of centuries especially towards other Christians and the injustices of the Third World. In thinking of others we have forgotten ourselves and have lost our identity in the Babylon of modern society. We are no longer different and have even thrown away our uniforms – you can't tell a nun any more – to join the rabble which shouts 'on with the revolution'. No society in history, they claim, has jettisoned its spiritual empire as quickly as 'modern Catholics' led by Pope John XXIII and Pope Paul VI.

The Church, they say, has lost much that is beautiful and holy; the mystique has gone out of religion and so Mass has become a jolly meal with the celebrant promising something new, something different next Sunday. It is the age of the gimmick and the 'do-it-yourself' congregation which saddens the Catholic who stands helplessly by as his beautiful churches are turned into dance halls at the offertory, wholesale talking shops at the sign of peace, and self-service cafeterias at communion. Suddenly there is a plurality of views in a Church to which previously you either conformed through absolute obedience or left as a heretic. The liturgy which was the focus of our unity is now the cause of division. There is a sort of despairing regret for the past today among older Catholics, many of them converts, who are praying in hope rather than anticipation for a return to the old Tridentine Mass and all that went with it. They are the sad people whom the Barque of Peter left stranded on the quayside as it headed for the high seas away from the safety of the harbour.

A few years ago I was at the bedside of a dying convert and I was grieved to hear his bitterness spill over on the Church which had thrown away all those things for which he had joined it. He did not want any ministrations but only those of a true Tridentine priest. Did he, a loyal supporter of the old Mass, die outside the Church? God give him peace.

While I do not agree with the attitude of these people especially when it engages in vitriolic abuse of the contemporary Church, nevertheless they have been treated shabbily. Our attitude towards them should not be to extricate ourselves from an awkward situation which could result in schism or, indeed, to avoid greater scandal than that which has already been given, but to bind up their wounds and give them back those sacred devotions which meant so much to their spiritual lives. Parishes are there to cater for the spiritual needs of all the people. It is pointless to talk of dialogue and plurality if we do not afford the same privilege in practice. Complete uniformity in forms of worship is due to the old preconciliar way of thinking. One non-productive claim for the Latin Mass is its use in universal places of pilgrimage. While that may be true and should be catered for, it is the normal local Sunday worship which brings the community in the 'here and now' together. Have we really been sincere in liturgical renewal? I know many clerics of all ranks who say Mass in English with as much meaning as a robot emitting its computerized messages. Uniformity has certainly given a shattering blow to our unity as Catholics – or were we just conformists all the time?

Vatican II is the scapegoat for all those who blame the mishaps in the Church on its influence. Catholics and those outside its fold tend to forget the clamour there was for change and reform before the Council. If it had not been summoned when it was then Europe would have been plunged into schism. I was very aware of this from my vantage point in Rome in the critical years preceding the Council. I remember attending a long seminar for South American bishops called by Pope Pius XII when the Bishops were adamant that everything in their garden was beautiful. They had no problems with the state as they were identified with it, while ecumenism for them was non-existent. It was a tawdry affair and a real eye-opener for me as a young clerical student. The bishops were engaging in a cover-up and Pope Pius XII would have none of it. He personally intervened to change the mood of the seminar and the bishops. Today South America is in the vanguard of Church thinking on pastoral strategy and has a great deal to offer our Church and world. South America needed the Council and vice versa.

Matters were coming to a head, especially in the liturgical field, and Pope Pius XII read the signs of the times quite clearly. It took Pope John's vision to call the Council which he could not finish and Pope Paul's courage and efficiency to finish what he could not have begun. Vatican II steered the forces for renewal into positive channels from which the whole Church benefited. I believe that the upheavals in the Church were already there long before the Council and those who were not aware of this were living in a dream world or a theological backwater. There is no going back to the past and the dead must be left to bury the dead.

That the vast majority of the laity did not know what was happening in the Church throughout the world was due, not so much to *suppressio veri* (withholding the truth), but to the underlying principle that the laity did not need to know anyway since decisions did not lie in their hands. If the laity had been better informed, then the changes would have taken place more smoothly and effectively. Cardinal Newman was once reprimanded by Rome for his pamphlet 'On consulting the Laity in Matters of Faith' but what he wrote then is still relevant today. We need an active lay voice in the Church if we are to grow to our full potential. The laity are still being told what to think and do even though in recent years they have been less prepared to listen. Pope Paul VI was a great champion of the laity. It was the Pope and the laity who saved the Church after the Council of Nicaea and it may well have to be so again.

People say that Vatican II was a failure and weakened the Church. I believe the Council would have made an even greater impact in the Church's history in our time, but tragically we were in general not ready for it in our country. It was a Council of vision and challenge but its message has gone out to the various parts of the world where we find clergy and laity clinging to old beliefs and practices which they regard as essential to their faith but are, in fact, in open contradiction to the teaching of the Council. On the other hand, equally destructive of the Council were those bishops and priests who followed the letter of the decrees and forgot the spirit. In other words they killed the Council in their areas before it had time to get off the ground. The Church was too scattered and conformist to decipher the true message of the Council, so that in some countries it became a cause for dissension long before it became a source of renewal. Preparation for renewal was just not adequate enough in these islands, but then there was no machinery which could be used to prepare both priests and people. This was soon remedied with the founding of pastoral centres whose work, I believe, has only begun to take effect.

God inspired the ideas of Vatican II but their formulation was left to the bishops confined in the hothouse atmosphere of the Vatican. The Council was at its worst an enormous teach-in with its consequent defects. One cynic described it as a 'brainwash of bishops' who returned to their senses after a period of convalescence in their own dioceses. We remember, of course, the Orthodox Church's reaction to the Council of Florence. When the Orthodox bishops returned to their dioceses they repudiated what they had signed. The implementation of Vatican II today has not been an easy task or time for the Pope or the Bishops and we must encourage them with all the people of God to press forward with renewal.

Cardinal Heenan in his book *Crown of Thorns* admitted that the bishops of this country were not prepared for the Council. They were out of touch with continental theological thinking and had allowed themselves over the years to slip into a backstream, so that very little positive, creative thinking found its way into the mainstream of our Catholic pastoral approach. We needed another Cardinal Newman at the Council and a Charles Borromeo afterwards to put it into effect in our island. It is one thing to dream dreams and quite another to make them come true. Councils do not come to realization by a wave of an ecclesiastical wand nor by sheer weight of bureaucratic commissions. The Council for some has become in more ways than one 'a paper tiger'. It is the advertisement we put in the window, even though the articles have not yet come off the production line. The Council has not yet sparked itself off as it should have done and the impetus is waning, even though efforts are made with a great amount of industry and good will. What is missing is the spirit of the Council's message which cannot be legislated for. It is, like the Council itself, a gift of the Holy Spirit to which we should all be open. We have to pray for renewal for all God's people; we cannot legislate for it.

The Church has always been changing down through the ages because all growth means change. The seed must die and the tree must be pruned if there is to be a bearing of fruit. If we want to live right in the heart of the Church we will realize that change is here to stay; the permanent force which remains with us all the time is the Holy Spirit. The Church is challenging rather than comforting and tells us to move on where we would like to put down roots. There has been controversy in the Church from the very beginning as regards the interpretation of Christ's will. Peter was criticized for eating with pagans and had to give an account of his conduct. 'The apostles and the brothers in Judaea heard that the pagans too had accepted the word of God, and when Peter came up to Jerusalem the Jews criticized him and said, "So you have been visiting the uncircumcized and eating with them, have you?" (Acts 11:1–3). Peter gave a detailed explanation of how he had baptized Cornelius and other pagans because he had seen the Holy Spirit come down on them:

> I had scarcely begun to speak when the Holy Spirit came down on them in the same way as it came on us at the beginning, and I remembered that the Lord had said: 'John baptised with water, but you will be baptised with the Holy Spirit.' I realised then that God was giving them the identical thing he gave to us when we believed in the Lord Jesus Christ; and who was I to stand in God's way? This account satisfied them, and they gave glory to God. *'God'* they said *'can evidently grant even the pagans the repentance that leads to life.'* (Acts 11:1–4,15–18)

The Jews realized for the first time how God was not their exclusive property but belonged to all those who were willing to receive the Spirit. This acceptance by them is far more radical than anything put forward by Vatican II. Do we really believe that God has stopped speaking to us and that we are not still a listening and learning people on the pilgrim's road? God speaks to us today in Vatican II and we must be prepared to listen and change our ways of thinking and acting. We are afraid of change because we are afraid to abandon our old positions. We have such a fear of falling that the moment of letting go is an act of trust. The only great virtue which sustains us is faith; we believe we can but fall into the hands of a loving Father. If we let go of those things which so bind us to the past that we cannot move forward into the future, then we will be a joy to our world and Church. Our conversion will continue to flow again as we are being converted every day. I appreciate how difficult it is to leave the sources of our spiritual riches behind and climb to even greater heights of holiness. We will not lose anything in the process so why are we afraid of change? Together we can renew the world if we allow the Spirit to lead us.

I believe that at the present time we can only appeal to Vatican II as an idealistic pattern towards which we must strive by a gradual process of prayer, dialogue, learning and listening. The Council has shown up our inadequacies as Christians in so far as it has been too often the cause of dissension. This has shown us how we all fall short of the ideal. Through the Council many priests, religious and laity were given a vision of their Church as it might be and they liked what they saw. Unfortunately many were not prepared to respond to its challenge. They wanted the edelweiss without climbing the mountain. It takes a long time to change people's attitudes especially if they are entrenched in their way of life.

Change involves growth and a certain dying. At the moment we are dying to the old structures and it is a very painful process. Our Lord's first recorded command to us is 'repent and believe the Good News' (Mark 1:15). We have to be converted in our hearts and turn from our old ways before we can accept the Good News. Without this transformation our lives will remain sterile and closed to God's loving message. We require a true *metanoia* – conversion – before we can live out the Council. There is something in us which shrinks from change, especially changing ourselves. Now it is about changing ourselves that the Council spoke and stiff resistance was only to be expected from all ranks and ages. When we 'repent' as Catholics, then the Good News will come alive for us in a new way. The Council documents are saturated with quotations from the Bible and once more we are reminded that we are a pilgrim people who live in tents. Vatican II was a pilgrim's 'Magna Carta'.

That we live in a pluralistic world is not a catch-phrase. Everything is changing round us with such increasing acceleration that ours is called the nomadic age in which people are afraid to put down roots. In recent times we have been taught some very salutary lessons in this country. Nine years ago in 1970 there was an uproar when leading Catholic theologians and laity suggested that we should look into the value of Catholic education. Two years previously in 1968 the encyclical 'Humanae Vitae' was published and in 1973 inflation hit our shores. Our schools are seriously affected. I see this as God's hand not wreaking vengeance but asking us to read the signs of the times:

> He said to the crowds, 'When you see a cloud looming up in the west you say at once that rain is coming, and so it does. And when the wind is from the south you say it will be hot, and it is. Hypocrites! You know how to interpret the face of the earth and sky. How is it that you do not know how to interpret these times?' (Luke 12:54–6)

God speaks in our times and we should *listen* to his voice in the world. I do not agree with those who say that we are such a teaching Church that we have nothing to learn from the world or from others. We have to learn to listen more, and yet we dare not just sit by and watch the changes in history when God means us to have an active part in these changes. We are Christians for today and now and not just to pay reverence to a past age. We have new frontiers to cross, above all within ourselves, so that if we slip back into the world of yesterday which has neither meaning nor relevance for our world then we are failures.

Change in the most creative sense is for Christians. The Council was not so much about changing structures as about changing people's lives and attitudes. We

67

should appreciate how much time and patience this involves. We can all count our battle scars from the Council but 'those who lay abed and did not fight with us will think themselves accursed'. It took courage to launch the Council and it needs it even more to keep it on course, if not always at full steam ahead. We are all suffering change together in the Church from the Pope to the person in the pew. We have a vision and courage born of faith and we refuse to be overcome. We must help those who have been damaged by the process of renewal and who can only see its faults without any of its fruits. Perhaps we pushed renewal of the Church for its own sake without taking the people into consideration enough. There can be no renewal of the Church or its liturgy without a renewal of the lives and spirit of the people.

Renewal means love of God and a deep concern about the feelings of individuals. Many people felt lost in all the changes because they identified themselves almost completely with Church structures. This is particularly true of priests and nuns who left their special calling in the Church in what can only be described as an exodus. Their leaving was a shock to everyone and caused great distress and heart searching. International figures of priests applying for laicization are extremely high and even these only take into account those who have bothered to apply for legislation of their status through ecclesiastical dispensation. The indifferent do not bother, as they want nothing more to do with the Church. There are no figures available in this country, but they too must be discouraging for those who feel it is their duty to withhold the information for what they consider genuine pastoral reasons. Priests who leave diminish us all, yet even after years of priests leaving the ministry, it takes courage to stand up and ask the questions 'How many?' and 'Why?'.

It is a cause of concern for us all and we must share the

blame and enquiry together. There is no point in sweeping the dust under the carpet if in the process we lose credibility in our own eyes. We need to know from priests who leave our ranks why they have chosen to do so and how they now see their future contribution to the Church. Many of them can enrich us and themselves instead of disappearing into the shadows of anonymity. We need to use their years of training and expertise. Thank God something is being done along these lines today in this country.

I am also concerned about the lives and mentality of the priests who find change extremely difficult and painful. Many are damaged by the changes affecting the essential fabric of their lives, even though few would be prepared to admit it. They believe that the martyr's crown is won by those who grin and bear it. I have profound compassion for them and know that beneath the surface there are deep hidden fears. They obey instructions but basically their hearts are not in all the changes. They were programmed for another age and another Church and they are trying to cope while more and more young priests leave their ranks. Security in old age is no longer certain or looked for even though increasing numbers retire at sixty-five, whereas previously the parish priest was expected to die in harness. No one has bothered to make really thorough enquiries to find out what the older clergy feel about the changes. I have no hesitation in saying quite simply that all is not well.

Many of my closest friends who had a very special contribution to make to the Church's renewal have now left our ranks. It is quite false to soothe our consciences by pretending that marriage was already in their sights when they started to 'criticize' the Church's structures. True, many subsequently married but this is the most natural thing to be expected of them. We are less equipped today to deal with Vatican II and renewal than we were a decade ago. If we all had been more open to the

Spirit of the Council, then we would have received their contribution with gladness and not suspicion. Renewal will be longer and more painful without them. They were not all 'saints' nor highly intelligent but a very high proportion of them were. One priest put it to me succinctly, 'We have lost relatively few; only the best'. Some wrote their books and cleared off the scene rather than allow themselves to be subjected to the ecclesiastical fusillade that was bound to follow. They had their entrances and their exits.

Many were impatient with the slowness of change, coupled with the distrust which their actions engendered in their superiors. They lacked what I call 'stickability'; the courage to keep going like water dripping on the rock and refusing to give up. We are not all made that way and the more sensitive yielded ground, rather than face the critical onslaught of intransigent factions which seem to delight when yet another 'radical' priest bites the dust. I am not exonerating them from all blame but where is the charity of Christ in all this? The sweetness of his wine has gone sour:

Let me sing to my friend
the song of his love for his vineyard.

My friend has a vineyard
on a fertile hillside.
He dug the soil, cleared it of stones,
and planted choice vines in it.

In the middle he built a tower,
he dug a press there too.
He expected it to yield grapes,
but sour grapes were all that it gave.

And now, inhabitants of Jerusalem
and men of Judah,

I ask you to judge
between my vineyard and me.
What could I have done for my vineyard
that I have not done?
I expected it to yield grapes.
Why did it yield sour grapes instead?

(Isaiah 5:1–4)

Some left – I do not know what proportion – because
they honestly believed they could do more for Christ
outside the priestly ministry. That they are doing so is an
incontrovertible fact and I know many 'ex-priests' who
are exercising a much more fruitful apostolate now than
they ever did in the ministry. What is God saying to us in
this? Is it not that there is a world to be won for him
maybe in ways we never visualized? Our task, instead of
worrying about 'mishaps' within our own structures, is to
go out and win our world with free minds and hearts.

The integrity of these men is beyond question and the
same I am sure could be said of women who were for-
merly religious. We need to give God thanks for their
witness instead of falling into the trap of the Pharisees.
They need our love and support; I want theirs. We have
all suffered and what a wonderful thing it would be if we
were to announce a year of reconciliation for former
priests and religious. We are all members of the same
Church whose bond is charity and whose cornerstone is
Christ:

You are God's chosen race, his saints; he loves you,
and you should be clothed in sincere compassion, in
kindness and humility, gentleness and patience. Bear
with one another; forgive each other as soon as a quar-
rel begins. The Lord has forgiven you; now you must
do the same. Over all these clothes, to keep them
together and complete them, put on love. And may the
peace of Christ reign in your hearts, because it is for

71

> this that you were called together as parts of one body.
> Always be thankful. (Col. 3:12–15)

The Church for which I was ordained a priest twenty-eight years ago is still the Bride of Christ and I love her, warts and all. I have, however, seen disagreements and an internal struggle which I would never have thought possible in Christ's community of faithful people. I am not intimidated by power nor discouraged by temporary setbacks; temporary because the kingdom of God will prevail. The Church of Christ is our source of inspiration and lifts up our eyes to new horizons. We are the priests, servants of God's mysteries and we do not leave in time of crisis. We stay within structures in order to renew people with Christ's vision and grace; they in turn will renew what is necessary in structures. We should get on with our main task of living our Christian lives. The true Church is only being partially obscured by those who are fighting a rearguard action. In love we want them to throw down their arms of hostility and suspicion. Only God can win the battle for people's hearts and he is winning every day, if only we look round us with eyes of faith and hope.

We have been chosen by God to live at one of the most exciting stages in man's history. The year 2000 is not so far away and many people wonder what it will bring. There are prophets of doom (or realists?) who tell us that our natural resources are nearly exhausted so that the sea-bed is our last hope for survival. The next decade will see changes of such a nature in our environment that the Church will be sucked into the maelstrom as man struggles for his survival and identity. The Church will change through force of circumstances and I believe that the Spirit of God is in these circumstances. The destiny of man and of the Church are intertwined perhaps as never before. We have a glorious opportunity as Christians to preach simply the gospel of Jesus without any of the trimmings. As pilgrims we cannot carry too much extra weight. Perhaps we will be sent another St Francis in love with people and all creation to lead us on our journey.

Time is neither for nor against us: it is with us:

There is a season for everything, . . .

A time for giving birth,
a time for dying;
a time for planting,
a time for uprooting what has been planted.
A time for killing,
a time for healing;
a time for knocking down,
a time for building.
A time for tears,
a time for laughter;
a time for mourning,
a time for dancing.
A time for throwing stones away,
a time for gathering them up;
a time for embracing,
a time to refrain from embracing.
A time for searching,
a time for losing;
a time for keeping,
a time for throwing away.
A time for tearing,
a time for sewing;
a time for keeping silent,
a time for speaking.
A time for loving,
a time for hating;
a time for war,
a time for peace.

(Ecclesiastes 3:1–8)

We need to understand what our time is calling us to. I believe it is *a time for searching*: it is certainly not one of uniformity. The plurality or fragmentation of our society is more able to have dialogue with a Church which is truly Catholic. We may have many voices within the Church but they will be united in harmony through love, or they should be, if we tried to live as Christians. Religious cynics say this is not possible, but then their estimation of God's love is so low as to make it non-existent.

Why is it that all Christians do not hear the Spirit calling for change in our age? Perhaps it is because they are in situations so secure as to remain aloof from reality. They do not hear the truth and do not want to since it would disturb them. Nothing must be allowed to rock the boat, and if a gale blows up, then the hatches are battened down while they ride out the storm.

There are others today in the Church, however, who see no hope of any meaningful change or leadership in the present structures. They need to lift up their eyes again to the God who makes all things new. We have every reason to hope. All the changes that have taken place in the Church over the centuries have a meaning which for the time were hidden from human understanding. The pains, misunderstandings, recriminations, doubts, sense of betrayal and everything associated with change today will be our Church 'groaning in one great act of giving birth' (Rom. 8:22) to a renewed Church. This age is glorious and that is why it is costing us so dearly. We have to break through the prison bars of convention and proclaim the freedom of the Lord. This is the alchemy of prophecy. We have a vision which we want to share:

Then I saw a new heaven and a new earth; the first heaven and the first earth had disappeared now, and there was no longer any sea. I saw the holy city, and the new Jerusalem, coming down from God out of heaven, as beautiful as a bride all dressed for her husband. Then I heard a loud voice call from the throne, 'You see this city? Here God lives among men. He will make his home among them; they shall be his people, and he will be their God; his name is God-with-them. He will wipe away all tears from their eyes; there will be no more death, and no more mourning or sadness. The world of the past has gone. (Rev. 21:1–4)

5. Is God really my Father?

I watched John die. His life, like his death, was tragic.
He was a winsome baby but he had a congenital disease
which meant that he would never be healthy or robust
like other children. His mother was dead and his father
who wanted to remarry and emigrate did not wish to be
burdened with an ailing child. So John was given into
care and now he belonged to whoever wished to adopt
him. Prospective parents came and went but his medical
record put people off. Everyone felt sorry for him but he
was too big a risk to adopt as one of the family.

He was different from the other children and was not
able for the rough and tumble of the orphanage. He
looked so sad sitting in the corner of the big playroom
that I had no option but to take him to my heart. I was a
young starry-eyed priest in my first parish and in John I
found a soul mate. Parish life was not what I expected
and the presbytery where I lived was, indeed, rather a
grim place. It is small wonder that John and I gave each
other mutual support as he swung off the end of my long
black cassock. Any happiness I could give this child
helped me over the stormy path of the mistakes of which
young priests are guilty or presumed guilty. John and I
had a lot in common. Whatever we did we were promptly
told to stop. Such is the price of individuality in institutions.

I spent hours with him, much to the displeasure of those who thought I had my priorities wrong. There were more valuable things to be done in an expanding city parish than playing games like an overgrown schoolboy with orphans – or so I was told – but these hours are for me precious memories; I would do exactly the same if I had my life to live all over again. John soaked up affection like a dried-up sponge plunged into water. He gave me more than I could possibly have given to him. John taught me a love for children which has always remained with me. In that sense he lives on in me.

To write off the weak and unwanted would mean not only the end of the Christian community but the end of the human race. Strong and healthy people need the weak and under-privileged so that they can become more human and loving. Jean Vanier, whose life is given to helping physically and mentally handicapped children, reminds us that perhaps with our greed and selfishness we are the 'abnormal' people of this world.

Soon I was dispatched to Rome to teach philosophy to future priests while John graduated up the scale to orphanages for older children who had not the good fortune to be adopted. He was surrounded by the wonderful Christian concern of religious sisters who had dedicated their lives to the selfless care of children, but he obviously missed the special love of someone who as a father would love him as his own. This I could never really supply as a priest, since we are here to love everyone and John had to make his own way in life. I have since met many lonely people like John in my life. Loneliness is no respecter of ages or persons. Geriatric hospitals can be like orphanages if there is no one to provide personal care. When John died the doctor diagnosed pneumonia. In reality he died of a broken heart because years before he was abandoned by his father. He belonged especially to no one, nobody wanted him.

When he died my faith in a loving God was put to the

test. I asked, 'Why, Lord, why? Why do these things happen and why do you allow such an innocent life to fade away like this before it has really begun to blossom? In our world there are many ungrateful children who have everything in life and yet John, who never really wronged anyone, is dying because he has not the will to live. Even the atheistic doctor says it is such a waste of a life. The odds were stacked against the poor youngster right from the start. It is such a cruel world that it is hard to believe, in moments as tragic as these, that there is someone out there who really cares. Never mind about the "problem of pain" or the "problem of sin". Whose sin was this? John's or his father's? Is this what human life is all about? Do I survive because I am one of the lucky ones? And what of life after death when there was so little one could call "life" on earth? Why did John come into our world at all?'

With the hindsight of the passing years I now understand things better than I did. I still do not fully grasp the anomalies of life where the good suffer and the wicked prosper. It is useless to pretend that we have all the answers. John died because our world is basically selfish. We pick out too often the healthy babies as the wanted ones and abandon the weak ones to orphanages and institutions. Our world cries out about 'unwanted' babies because in its selfishness it is afraid of life and the consequences of unselfish love. John's father denied him his birthright and, even though his reasoning as to his own future marriage was logical, he forgot to love his sick child. He did not commit a crime against society but only against his son. John was meant for his father's love and he just could not live without it.

I know where the blame lies. The only thing I would lay at God's door is that he has not taken away our freedom to hurt others. Too often we make God the scapegoat for our own failure to use our freedom fully and responsibly in our attitude towards others, especially those who should be nearest and dearest to us. Yet if God took away our freedom we would not be human. Sin would be impossible. Michel Quoist reminds us in his best-selling book *Prayers of Life* that 'sin is disorder and disorder hurts. There is for every sin, somewhere in the world and in time, a corresponding suffering. And the more sins there are, the more suffering'. Yet without freedom we could not love. Fathers love their sons because they want to and not because they have to. You cannot make people love. There is no state law which would send John's father to gaol for not loving his son. If there were then we would have to build large prisons in every city in the world to house 'unloving' parents.

Freedom to be ourselves in the best sense of the word is when we do not place ourselves at the centre of our universe. The vowel 'i' is in the centre of sin and indeed of all selfishness when our 'ego' becomes blown up into a capital 'I'. We are free when we say 'yes' because we are able to say 'no'. John's father in fact said 'yes' to himself and the life he wanted to lead, even though it meant saying 'no' to his young child. He was acting like a Roman emperor in the game of life when he gave the thumbs down to his son. He could not have it both ways and so was guilty of the sin as old as the one committed by the first parents to walk our earth — self before others no matter what the consequences.

That is not the way God treats his children:

I myself taught Ephraim to walk,
I took them in my arms;
yet they have not understood that I was the one
looking after them.
I led them with reins of kindness,
with leading-strings of love.
I was like someone who lifts an infant close against his
cheek;

79

stooping down to him I gave him his food. (**Hosea** 11:3–4

God loves us as a father but it is hard to see him as a father when the one to whom we have so much love to give deliberately chooses to walk out of our lives. 'I will not abandon you', God reassures us time and again from the pages of the Bible:

> 'Does a woman forget her baby at the breast,
> or fail to cherish the son of her womb?
> Yet even if these forget,
> I will never forget you.' (Isaiah 49:15)

Jesus, too, calls us his friends and promises, 'I will not leave you orphans' (John 14:18).

Jesus, even though he freely died for us, cried out on the Cross: 'My God, my God, why have you deserted me?' (Mark 15:34). We do not understand suffering because we have failed to appreciate the sacrifices involved in total love. We cannot blame God for man's freedom to sin. We are all free to refuse God's love. Because God is *pure* love he leaves us at liberty through his great respect for us, even when we lose respect for him. His infinite respect for what he has made – man the peak of creation – means that he is the only lover who gives to those he loves the fullest possible freedom. All other love is a reflection of God's love. Freedom is as much a mystery as a gift which we can use or abuse. 'I am free', writes Juan Arias, 'when I believe in a God who will not repent of having created me free.' When we hurt each other we are not acting as the children of God's family who were meant to live in love and harmony. God could not step in and stop us hurting each other without taking away the basis of our human nature which is freedom. Our Christian faith is the religion of freedom and it is the most precious gift offered to us by Jesus Christ. Yet freedom like love is one of the most abused words in modern language. I cannot use either to my own advantage at the expense of others.

We come to God through people. John's unhappiness is sadly becoming more typical of our modern world. It is more difficult today to talk about God as a loving father when so many have little or no experience of love in their home life. I am sorry for parents of broken marriages but I weep for their children. They are the victims of the very cruel violence of not being loved by the very ones who brought them into the world. If our lives are sordid, selfish and lonely, if we are the Scrooges who say out upon everything that smacks of Christmas goodwill, then it is hardly ever likely that we shall find a loving God, much less a Father who wants to share his own life with us. If we Christians do not show him to those with whom we come in contact, then he will remain for them the unknown God.

Mahatma Gandhi admitted he was impressed by the life of Christ but not by the life of Christians. The world would have believed long ago if we in the Church had lived as we should have done. We all bear the collective guilt for the world's atheism. 'The world does not reproach us for being Christian,' writes Cardinal Suenens, 'but for not being Christian enough. We must be powerful Christians not timid ones.' The Church is there for mission to the world and not almost exclusively to its own élite.

The reason Jesus came on earth as one of us was to show us in his personality the true and only way to the Father. At the Last Supper Jesus told his disciples about his imminent passion, death and resurrection, and how he was going to prepare a place for his followers in his Father's house:

'I am the Way, the Truth and the Life.
No one can come to the Father except through me.

81

If you know me, you know my Father too.
From this moment you know him and have seen him.'

Philip said, 'Lord, let us see the Father and then we shall be satisfied'. 'Have I been with you all this time, Philip,' said Jesus to him, 'and you still do not know me?

'To have seen me is to have seen the Father,
so how can you say, "Let us see the Father"?
Do you not believe
that I am in the Father and the Father is in me?'

(John 14:6–10)

That the child is the father of the man is no platitude. We are all indebted to our family and friends for giving us so much that is of value, spiritually, in our lives. We live under the sway of their influence and it is only when we look back in later years that we appreciate the significance of all that they contributed so selflessly to whatever is noble in our lives. They have passed across our stage but what they said and did has now become inextricably part of who and what we are. They would be amazed if we were to begin to tell them of our surpassing gratitude to them.

My own parents were vintage Irish Catholics and I could ask for no finer start in life. My Christian faith began when at the age of two days I was carried in my father's arms to be baptized in Saints Peter and Paul's Church in Cork. The seed for making peace and unity among all peoples was first planted in my heart when I saw the love of my mother for people of all denominations and none. No Christmas Day went by without a tramp or two to share our festive meal. Her gentleness filled our home and the memory of her quietly slipping out to morning mass at six o'clock on the first Friday of every month has always stayed with me. She remained a country girl with all the nobility that only contact with the soil can give. She spent hours with us and was always at home. I remember running home from the school at term's end to tell her everything that happened and as we shared I watched her eyes light up. My father, artistic and bohemian in temperament, was a born mimic and storyteller. The evenings round the huge fire and the piano are happy memories which mellow with the years. Poetry, art and music were his loves and he was at all times a man of peace. He abhorred violence and bigotry. In later years he was saddened by events in Northern Ireland. He was one of us, a big brother, who spent hours with us and took part in all our joys and sorrows. He ruled by love and not by compulsion. Is it any wonder that I believe so easily that God is love and is my Father?

Even though faith is God's gift, nevertheless we come to a realization of what a living faith really means through people and the Holy Spirit. A loving community of the Christian family is the perfect seeding ground for receiving the word of God. I learned more about God's love from my parents than I did from any seminary professor or from the study of ecclesiastical documents. Explanations of doctrine were addressed to my mind and I found as much satisfaction in understanding them as I did in solving mathematical problems or a jigsaw puzzle. They remained on the level of theory – a purely intellectual exercise. I 'caught' the faith from my parents as truly as I did my Irish brogue.

Our faith was a way of life in our family. One day we will meet merrily in heaven and this thought has often kept me going when the days are dark and the going rough. The institutional Church has given me a great deal and I am a loving part of it, but it is my parents above all to whom I owe my love and allegiance. The break-up of family life is in fact the erosion of our full lives as human beings and a distortion of our approach to a loving God. The institutional Church that forgets itself and puts the family first in its list of priorities is coming close to the mind of God our Father from whom every family, whether spiritual or natural, takes its name.

No institutional Church can ever take the credit for our faith. True, it may help it to grow but it can also diminish it. An institution, however highly motivated by its principles, tends to put itself first in the order of priorities for loyalty and service. The bigger the institution, the more depersonalized it becomes. My parents and those who have lived the Christian life have helped me to grow as a person who tries to follow Jesus Christ, and it is their example which has facilitated my joyful acceptance of faith in the Church. If I love Christ and his Church, then this is due to a large extent to the fact that it meant so much to them. Such it seems is God's plan, at least in my case, for knowing and loving him.

My parents from my earliest years taught me that outgoing love to God and people, together with freedom to be myself, were the most important things in life. They showed by example what it was to allow God into my life. I experienced prayer and God's transforming love long before I ever read about them. My sisters and brother trained me for the world in the unique struggle for survival and for personal identity which only a large family can provide. My friends of all shades of belief and none helped me to find God or rather allowed him to find me. A television comedian, not universally popular with Roman Catholics, always ends his programme with the words: 'May *your* God go with you.' We all see God largely through other people's lives which have influenced us. The institutional Church which realizes that faith comes through people's love, and not its laws, will soon discover the power it has for beauty and belief in a world which wants to believe in someone or something which is generous and caring. I believe today because those I love have never ceased believing all down through the years. The light of faith has been faithfully passed on and now I hold the torch.

My God is the one revealed by Christ. My God is a rainbow God of many beautiful colours. He is not the preserve of Roman Catholics alone but belongs also to Anglicans, Methodists, Free Churchmen, Pentecostalists; he is the God of Sikhs, Muslims, Agnostics and every man who believes in someone bigger than himself.

God comes to us through people. He takes the initiative in faith. It is he who calls, often as gently as a breeze in a cool summer's evening, and we respond with our: 'Yes, I believe in You. I believe not only that you exist, but I believe in you because I see your work in my world. I see you in people's love and lives. I see you in my parents. I know what you have done and are doing in my life. I surrender my life to you in loving obedience because in this way I can become the sort of person you want me to become.'

Faith is always growing. Our belief is possible, therefore, only in so far as we are willing to listen and respond to God's call to grow in holiness and humanity. In this way our belief is maturing as we become more sensitive and eager to respond to God's life within us. I hope I have more faith today than I had this time last year.

God's call always makes us more ourselves since he is the author of all life. By freely opening ourselves to his love, we are allowing him to continue his work of creation in us in a new and beautiful way. My own faith is the ultimate support through which I can help others to believe. Perhaps the greatest service I can render to my world is, when in union with the Holy Spirit, I help, however minutely, to open people to the loving light of faith. In this way I am giving thanks to God for all he has given me in Christ through my parents and friends. I believe that the Christian faith is the most precious jewel which when we have we want to share. It may be that people do not want to accept it. What I pray is that they experience the joy of loving and being loved by God. If they miss out on that, then I shall still love them, even though I shall wonder why has God been so generous to me with his gifts of faith, family and friends.

We often fear that once we admit the existence of God and our total dependence on him we will not be able to lead an authentic human existence. We dread becoming puppets on the string of a divine manipulator. Vatican II reminds us that this fear is caused by 'the desire for human independence that is stretched to such a point that it poses difficulties against any kind of dependence upon God'. The scientific age in which man is told that he has all the answers necessary for his survival and growth tends to reject God. Man becomes autonomous and is drunk with the heavy wine of so-called 'freedom'. Yet, I have known at first-hand great scientists who openly confess their belief and dependence on him.

God in reality wants us to use all our skills and inventiveness to make the world a better place. He is not against modern science and as Christians we do not oppose what we view in science as the fulfilment of humanity. Our worldly values, ambitions and pleasures are not disapproved of by God except in so far as they make us less human, less alive. God loves everything that makes us ultimately happy. He is calling us to a perfection of life which transforms ordinary human existence and invites us to lead an enriched life. He desires what is best for us through what is best in us. His only son Jesus told us why he was sent on earth by his Father; 'I have come so that they may have life and have it to the full.' (John 10:10).

The fact that God sent his son to us is an endorsement of our humanity and the answer to our yearning to become whole persons. By his total involvement in our human situation Jesus frees us from the fear of a God who is a threat to our freedom and our development as full persons. God entered our human history and transformed our universe. Christ is the centre of the hour-glass

86

through which all time flows for purification and meaning. It is tragic when we view the world as divorced from God. He must have been pleased that we discovered atomic power as a source of energy and saddened that it was first used on a massive scale against human beings. Everything in the world is good when we use it properly with love and respect. When man is polluting and plundering his environment we as children of the universe should be 'friends of the earth' which was given to us as our heritage. We should wish to enjoy and conserve it for future generations.

If we analyse our fear of God, we will acknowledge that basically the reason why we do not love him is because we do not know him or what he wants for us. We reject in fact the 'God' who does not exist. We are afraid, too, of what loving God involves. We want to remain ourselves and we fear that God would want to change us if we committed ourselves to him. We hold on to what we have instead of daring to love and let go. Francis Thompson expressed this fear 'The Hound of Heaven':

> For though I knew His love who followed
> Yet was I sore adread
> Lest having Him I must have naught beside.

God, however, reassures the soul fleeing from his pursuit:

> All which I took from thee, I did but take
> Not for thy harms
> But just that thou mightest seek it in My arms.
> All which thy child's mistake
> Fancies as lost, I have stored for thee at home:
> Rise, clasp My hand and come.

If God is pure love then his relationship with us will be total. He wants our response to him to be the same even though it will take a lifetime to grow. When we surrender to him in love, a little timidly at first, We will begin to shed our fears, like a child who comes out of darkness into a wonderful new world of light – a real Alice in Wonderland. 'To discover God', writes Dom Bede Griffiths, 'is not to discover an idea but to discover one-self. It is to awake to that part of one's existence which has been hidden from sight and which one has refused to recognize. The discovery may be very painful; it is like going through a kind of death. But it is the one thing that makes life worth living.' We may have kept God up to now at a safe and respectable distance; perhaps even through the motions of religion and the mumbo jumbo of 'prayer' which has become a spell to frighten away evil spirits. We stay out of the deep waters of deep faith lest we drown. But isn't that what the waters of baptizm were meant to be – a drowning to the old self and a new birth in Christ? We die in baptizm to all our fears and these we bury with Christ in the old tomb of self, so that we can emerge as a new creation. 'You have been taught that when we were baptized in Christ Jesus we were baptized in his death; in other words, when we were baptized we went into the tomb with him and joined him in death, so that as Christ was raised from the dead by the Father's glory, we too might live a new life' (Rom. 6:3–4).

God loves us more than we love ourselves and yet we are afraid to trust ourselves to him. When we converse deeply with holy people who have experienced God in their lives, we will discover how human and unspoiled they are. They are completely themselves because they have given their lives over to God. Our Christian faith is all about loving with a love which casts out fear. Total love in human terms means in one sense that we are no longer ourselves but we find ourselves in another self. We are two in one. It is in this kind of love that we in fact discover our true, deeper selves. If we have never known human love, then how can we even begin to understand

God's love in all its thrilling generosity? He is vulnerable to us and we to him.

We do not trust ourselves to God's loving care for our destiny, because we find it difficult to believe that such a love exists anywhere in the world. It seems too good to be true since so many things seem to happen by chance. Yet God gets up an hour earlier than fate every morning! Our crisis in growth as individuals is a crisis of faith and hope. We do not believe in him and that is why we do not trust him. We prefer to manage our own lives and keep our hands on the helm, so that at least we can be sure of our future. We do not even begin to get a glimmer of what the word 'God' means, because we have never plumbed the depths of human love. We have not experienced the joy and pain of loving another for himself or herself alone. If the word 'love' means little to us, then God has no meaning. Husbands and wives in true married love give to the other totally, and would not have it otherwise. As soon as they decide to give only in so far as they receive, then their marriage is heading for the dangerous rocks of selfishness and destruction. We have not lived out, as Christians, our top priority, the true meaning of generous love, and this defect more than any other is the reason why people today are not prepared to believe in God. They are more impressed by lives than dogmas. Christ tells us how we are to witness to being his followers:

> I give you a new commandment:
> love one another;
> just as I have loved you,
> you also must love one another.
> By this love you have for one another,
> everyone will know that you are my disciples. (John 13:34–5)

If our lives were authentic, then the world would get a clearer image of who God really is. Juan Arias is quite clear about the God he does not believe in:

No, I shall never believe in:

the God incapable of giving an answer to the grave problems of a sincere and honest man who cries out in tears: 'I can't!'

the God who loves pain,

the God who makes Himself feared,

the God who does not allow people to talk familiarly to him,

the grandfather-God whom one can twist around one's little finger,

the God who makes Himself the monopoly of a church, a race, a culture or a caste,

the God who doesn't need man,

the judge-God who can give a verdict only with a rule book in His hands,

the God incapable of smiling at many of man's awkward mistakes,

the God who 'sends' people to hell,

the God who does not know how to hope,

the God who can be fully explained by a philosophy,

the God incapable of forgiving what many men condemn,

the God incapable of redeeming the wretched,

the God who prevents man from growing, and conquering,

the God who demands that if a man is to believe he must give up being a man,

the God capable of being accepted and understood by those who do not love,

the God who says 'You will pay for that!'

the God who sometimes regrets having given man free will,

the God who stifles earthly reform and gives hope only for the future life,

the God who puts law before conscience,

the God who has no forgiveness for some sins,

the God who 'causes' cancer or 'makes' a woman sterile,

the God who does not save those who have not known Him but who have desired and searched for Him,

the God who does not go out to meet him who had abandoned Him,

the God incapable of making everything new,

the God who does not have a different, personal, individual word for each person,

the God who has never wept for men,

the God who can not find Himself in the eyes of a child or a pretty woman or a mother in tears,

the God who destroys the earth and the things that man loves instead of transforming them,

the God who will accept as a friend anyone who goes through the world without making anybody happy,

the God incapable of making man divine and seating him at His table and giving him part of His heritage,

the God who is not love and who does not know how to transform into love everything He touches,

the God incapable of captivating man's heart,

the God who would not have become a man, with all that that implies,

the God who would not have given men even His very own mother,

the God in whom I cannot hope against all hope,

Yes, my God is the other God.

But how did we get this false notion of God? The blame lies in the way religion was taught in previous ages; a way which has done so much harm to people's spiritual lives by its emphasis on the wrath of God who will punish with untold tortures those who break his laws. Medieval art proves this point conclusively. No denomination is free from this charge of building up guilt complexes which paralysed people and gave rise to all sorts of abuses of true religion. Religion for many people is not related to life. Can we honestly say that our memories of religious services in our youth filled us with joy, or was Sunday service a bore demanded by an ever-watching tyrannical God? What was your experience? I can only tell you about mine.

The centre of my life for many years was dominated by the fear of falling into mortal sin which automatically cut me off from God. I saw God as a judge and I was literally terrified of hell about which I had many nightmares. Justification was achieved by personal effort so that life became increasingly full of tensions and anxieties. The big sin, of course, was sex and the sermon which attracted maximum attendance during a parish mission was the one which dealt with the evils of 'company keeping'. I have heard sermons preached which made us feel that our sins would have brought a blush to the cheeks of even the most hardened sinners of Sodom and Gomorrah. God became such a kill-joy that I compartmentalized religion until gradually it was reduced to a one-hour exercise to be undertaken on Sundays in my best clothes. It had nothing to do with life or being human.

We were proud of our differences from other Christians and we sang of 'dungeon, fire and sword', knowing at whose hands we suffered, long after the siege was over. It was all part of our heritage which we were not allowed to forget. Partisan loyalty was curiously mixed up with our belief so that it was impossible to distinguish one from the other. It was faith and fatherland of a limiting kind with all its consequences that may be so dire, when carried to extremes – as has happened in Northern Ireland. Religion remained on the periphery of my consciousness and I never allowed it for many years to penetrate the real 'me'.

I was not yet converted to the notion of a loving God even though my parents were so obviously fulfilled as

Catholics. I felt in some intangible way, which I could not analyse, that there must be something special in the Catholic faith, because of how much it meant to them. They were human, happy and the secret of it all lay in the fact that their religion was part and parcel of everything they were and did. I did not want to hurt them by opting out, even though I knew in my teens that many of my contemporaries had lapsed from the faith without any apparent evil consequences. But what did they lapse from? I believe it was from a parody and a caricature of who God really is. They did not in fact reject God but the monster who was presented to them.

'The fear of the Lord is the beginning of wisdom' (Prov. 7:7) was quoted to me time and again. I realized that: 'It is a dreadful thing to fall into the hands of the living God' (Heb. 10:31) so I stayed out of his reach as much as possible. Whatever the truth about heaven, I certainly knew there was a hell. I was happy because I did not allow religion to dominate my waking hours or enter my hobbies and pleasures. Religion at school was learned by rote, to be quoted by us at length in the same mechanical way as our multiplication tables, when we were questioned as to why we believed. It was mainly an intellectual exercise and the approach too apologetic, unreal and cold. We occasionally deliberated about God rather than lived for him. I cannot say that God was ever real for me at school, even though the Catholic Church in the person of the priest loomed so large in my life – as if to make God a second-best, or so it seemed to me. I am sure my teachers did not mean to do this, but it was in fact what they achieved by their teaching and attitude. They never let me forget that I was a Catholic and a member of the biggest religious denomination in the world. I could only be saved as a Catholic and to reject my faith was the unpardonable crime bringing shame on my entire family.

All that has now changed for me, but there are still

large numbers of all denominations who carry this image to the grave. Only recently an old woman suffering from a terminal disease was afraid of death precisely because of her wrong spiritual formation. She and I went through mental torture as I tried to unravel with her the knots which she had got herself into over the years. God has now revealed to her the wonders of his love and life as she lives at peace in his presence.

Today I am a different person. The change was brought about in me by the power of the Holy Spirit. Once I allowed Christ to live in me then my whole attitude to religion and life changed. The spirit of the Risen Christ released me from the tomb of my empty fears so that at last I could call God, 'Abba', Father:

> Everyone moved by the Spirit is a son of God. The spirit you received is not the spirit of slaves bringing fear into your lives again; it is the spirit of sons, and it makes us cry out, 'Abba, Father!' The Spirit himself and our spirit bear united witness that we are children of God. And if we are children we are heirs as well: heirs of God and coheirs with Christ, sharing his sufferings so as to share his glory. (Rom. 8:14–17)

The great gift Christ gives to us is to call God, 'Father'. He brought us a freedom of spirit which makes us glad that we are Christians. Our service is real freedom and 'When Christ freed us, he meant us to remain free. Stand firm, therefore, and do not submit again to the yoke of slavery' (Gal. 5:1).

Yet no look at fear would be complete without asking the question whether or not there is a legitimate fear of the Lord. The answer is quite simply this: theologians distinguish between *servile* and *filial* fear. Servile fear belongs to slaves who as guilty servants anticipate the just wrath and punishment of their master. Filial fear is the selfless fear of the lover who fears to hurt or lose the

Beloved, a fear seen at its highest in the saints. Jesus has said: '. . . I shall not call you servants any more, because a servant does not know his master's business; I call you friends, because I have made known to you everything I have learnt from my Father' (John 15:15). We are the friends of Jesus but more than that we are God's children: 'Think of the love that the Father has lavished on us, by letting us be called God's children; and that is what we are' (1 John 3:1).

Today the love of God is being preached, taught and lived by the Christian Churches more than has been done for generations. The growth of charismatic renewal has been a great source of release for the Churches, and it is not surprising that vast numbers flock to its prayer meetings in order to express their overpowering sense of God's love. Power-orientated and structure-conscious people are suspicious of those who have drunk the new wine: this is merely a situation in which the history of the first Pentecost repeats itself. The system that preaches fear rules by fear and, from my experience in the field of Christian unity, every denomination has been guilty of highlighting God's justice at the expense of his love and mercy. It was as if the Good News of the New Testament never happened.

When I began to read the life of Christ and the Early Church as if it was written personally for me, I realized how far we all had strayed from the basic, simple message that God is love and how he made us for himself. Love is the key that unlocks the Bible and the path that leads to fullness of life. What occurred in the early Church when God was so clearly the Father of his people can happen again, if only we see the gospel as a challenge to be lived out by us. We must repeat again and again that God is our Father and perhaps then the world will learn to believe. Now I can appreciate the beauty of the Roman Catholic faith without in any way diminishing the faith of other believers.

The greatest song of joy in the New Testament was spoken by Mary, the mother of Jesus. It was a revolutionary hymn which praised God for what he had achieved for his people: 'He has pulled down princes from their thrones and exalted the lowly. The hungry he has filled with good things, the rich sent empty away' (Luke 1:52–3). We who, before, were a disorganized rabble in conflict with one another as in Babylon, each going his own way, are welcomed as a new people to share God's home and love. We shout with joy that, 'His mercy reaches from age to age for those who fear him' (Luke 1:50) as we stand in awe, reverence and love before his throne. With the great assembly of the faithful I praise the Lord who has worked marvels for me, Holy his name. I know he was the One who was there all the years in my fearful wanderings through life. I am afraid no longer and ask him, 'May I call you Father?'

6.   Are you afraid to be yourself?

We are afraid to be ourselves. We dare not search the hidden parts of our personality lest, when they are discovered, they may threaten us with the stark reality of who we really are. We bury them beneath the surface of activity or self-excuse and promise never again to explore the deep recesses of our mysterious selves, lest we come face to face again with the skeleton in each of our cupboards. We become externalized 'people' living on the periphery of life, so that we avoid those occasions which confront us with ourselves. Yet until we have the courage to face up to who we really are, we will never come alive as persons. We cannot be happy on the outside without first being happy on the inside.

We often pray, 'Lord, deliver us from ourselves' without ever giving ourselves a chance to become the kind of person God wants us to become. The reason is obvious. We are not in love with who we are and we believe that in the final analysis we are basically unlovable. How or why God loves us – if we ever really believe it – will remain a mystery and we put it down to his mercy rather than to anything of value in ourselves. We reject in practice, although perhaps not consciously, God's creation in us. We consider that we are part of the sin of the world and so we limp through life without ever coming to grips with the reality which is 'me' in each of us.

We hide who we are from God, from others and above all from ourselves in the wilderness of the world we have made. 'Where are you?' God asks. 'I heard the sound of you in the garden', we reply, 'I was afraid because I was naked and so I hid.' 'Who told you that you were naked?' God asks and we have no reply. Fear has driven us into a situation of our own making. We have failed to come to terms with ourselves and, so, play the deadly destroying game of hide-and-seek with life.

We are forever asking the question, 'Who am I?' We may read numerous books on psychology and know all the answers in theory but the question of personal identity still remains unanswered. We never really square up to the question because we are afraid of the answer we might get. So we remain locked in on ourselves through fear, and the real self becomes even more frustrated as we refuse it an outlet for expression. We are at war within ourselves which is the perfect recipe for neurosis. Religion becomes our tranquillizer so that we can maintain an even keel in the troublesome sea of life. Tranquillizers never make for tranquillity. We become people addicted to our spiritual rocking chair which helps us to rest when we are restless. Our calm is on the surface while underneath the tensions build up to breaking point.

In over twenty-seven years of ministering to people I have found that failure to be themselves is the main cause of loneliness and despair in our world. It is the chief source of nervous breakdown and deep unhappiness. The fear to be ourselves is the most difficult emotion to control because we do not know of what we are afraid. Yet fear has to be faced up to and dragged out of the dark places where it lurks. When we see it in its proper light then we will appreciate what battles lie ahead if we are to have a personal identity. An enemy confronted is less terrible than unseen forces which in the background steadily erode our self-confidence. It is the obscure

98

menace which unnerves the mind. The nameless dread is put before us in a startling way in Coleridge's haunting image in *The Rime of the Ancient Mariner*:

Like one, that on a lonesome road
Doth walk in fear and dread,
And having once turned round walks on
And turns no more his head;
Because he knows a frightful fiend
Doth close behind him tread.

Our greatest fear is to recognize ourselves for what we are, lest not only are we rejected by others but that we too reject what we find. Self-rejection is destructive of any kind of personal growth. Self-analysis is a pain we would rather be without. So life becomes a dark menace which will engulf us in some future inevitable calamity. The seeds of destruction are within us, and we are afraid that they may grow one day to such proportions as to smother all the things in life we hold dear. We shrink from darkness and the elemental fear of being left totally alone: 'with darkness my one companion left' (Ps. 88).

Our hidden fears, when they are brought to light, lose their power over us. The frightened mind nearly always exaggerates the things we fear and conjures up in the imagination all sorts of calamitous happenings. The shadow of the cross is always larger than the cross itself when in the evening the day's light begins to fade. Fear lives in the land of shadows. Its territory is the night, which soon spills over into our waking hours so that life becomes total darkness. In this way fear is a force which blinds our self-perception and brings life to a standstill.

We fight fear as we fight physical disease. We should not merely ask ourselves the questions 'What am I afraid of in myself?' and 'Why?' but write down the questions and answers for future reflection and action. Fear hates to be confronted since it lives by innuendo and unspoken menace. It is the question mark which becomes the tombstone over our buried self. Like a vampire it sucks our life blood so that we have to unearth the coffin, open it and drive a stake through the heart of the demon fear. Only then will we find peace.

When we know our secret fears for what they are we can set about finding a remedy. Psychiatric help may be sought in exploring the subconscious and laying bare the origin of the things which stunt our human growth. But while psychology helps us to overcome fears, particularly those that are abnormal and phobic, nevertheless what we are really lacking in life is faith – faith in ourselves and faith in God. The old saying is still true:

> Fear knocked at the door.
> Faith answered.
> There was no one there.

Faith not only means that we believe in God but that we trust that he believes in us. The fact that God believes in me means that he knows that I am capable of totally fulfilling myself. To have faith in God without believing that he has faith in us is to deny that we are Christians. We tend as Christians to minimize God's generosity to us simply because we have not allowed the Bible to come alive for us. We so exaggerate the need for our own belief in God (as if we could be saved by that aspect of faith alone), that we ignore the great virtue of hope by which we trust that God believes fully in me and in every human person. Hope like faith is the enemy and conqueror of fear. What we need today are large doses of hope. The Church that preaches hope will not be able to cater for the crowds that flock like parched children to drink in its message. Damnation is preached through fear, and heaven through hope.

When Christian hope is authentic, born of God's faith

in us manifested through Christ, then it is vigorous and life-giving. Christ came that we 'may have life and have it to the full' (John 10:10). It is our hope that keeps us joyful and sets us free from the shackles of fear which keep us chained in the dark dungeons of self-doubting. Hope tells us that what remains to be done with the rest of our lives will be done, and that what we have spoiled will be transformed in the life and light of our Risen Lord. Christ has overcome the world of sin and selfishness and the victory which is ours for the taking has already been won. Life has conquered death and the tomb of self is broken leaving only the bandages which bound our eyes of inward faith and hope. We are not to seek the living among the dead. We are not in the tomb. We are risen with him to walk in the morning air.

We need to convince ourselves that 'by turning everything to their good God co-operates with all those who love him' (Rom. 8:28). St Paul was convinced of the power of Christ: 'There is nothing I cannot master with the help of the One who gives me strength' (Phil. 4:13). The Bible is full of images that inspire confidence in the love of God the Father for his children. 'Do not take fright . . . Yahweh your God goes in front of you and will be fighting on your side as you saw him fight for you in Egypt. In the wilderness, too, you saw him: how Yahweh carried you, as a man carries his child, all along the road you travelled on the way to this place' (Deut. 1:30–1). If we take hope out of the Bible then what have we left?

Fear is basically a lack of faith and hope. We do not believe that God has the power to help us and, even if he did, we think that he doesn't really care anyway. We reason that since we got ourselves into the mess in which we find ourselves, then we will be left on our own to get ourselves out of it. What an insult to God! I remember talking to a woman who was all hung up on her approach to God. She was trying for perfection by her own efforts, an impossible and un-Christian task, and was appalled at her own weaknesses. I quoted Paul's prayer in his letter to the Ephesians:

> Out of his infinite glory, may he give you the power through his Spirit for your hidden self to grow strong, so that Christ may live in your hearts through faith, and then, planted in love and built on love, you will with all the saints have strength to grasp the breadth and the length, the height and the depth; until, knowing the love of Christ, which is beyond all knowledge, you are filled with the utter fullness of God.
>
> Glory be to him whose power, working in us, can do infinitely more than we can ask or imagine; glory be to him from generation to generation in the Church and in Christ Jesus for ever and ever. Amen. (Eph. 3:16–21)

She realized for the first time that God did not want her to face life alone but that he was with her in all things, sustaining and helping her. From the moment of realization her conversion began.

God cares for the individual as someone unique whom he loves. 'I have branded you on the palms of my hands,' (Isa. 49:16). He calls us by name out of the darkness into the light of his life. "Do not be afraid, for I have redeemed you/*I have called you by your name, you are mine*' (Isa. 43:1). Each one of us is infinitely precious to him. We may be expendable to institutions but God is not an institution. He is a Father who loves us and goes on loving us whether we acknowledge it or not. The Lord assures us: 'Can you not buy two sparrows for a penny? And yet not one falls to the ground without your Father knowing. Why, every hair on your head has been counted. So there is no need to be afraid; you are worth more than hundreds of sparrows' (Matt. 10:29–31). The Church of hope and trust which preaches the dignity and lovableness of every individual is the one which is faithful to the gospel of Christ. It will preach God's love in season and out of season.

We trust ourselves and our hidden selves in faith to the One whom we have never seen and whom we know only by faith. Faith and hope give us courage to face up to life and to ourselves. What is courage, but the power of life to affirm itself against all the odds? It is a positive refusal to be overcome. Christ and I are an absolute majority in any situation. We believe in his words. 'I am the light of the world; anyone who follows me will not be walking in the dark; he will have the light of life' (John 8:12). If we really believed that we are loved and watched over by a Person who is Love itself then how could we fear? Father Willie Doyle, an Irish Jesuit, was accosted one day by a prostitute. He reminded her that God loved her but she laughed at him. It was too good to be true. Years later in her prison cell she sent for him and was received into the Church. The simple statement 'God loves you' stayed with her in the intervening years to haunt her with its implications. Eventually she succumbed to the great truth and she, whose life was loveless and tawdry, was changed by the realization of God's powerful love. Love alone can transform us if only we allow it into our lives. God will not allow us to settle for second-best.

In all situations where we fall like the soul in 'The Hound of Heaven' 'adown Titanic glooms of chasmed fears', underneath us are the everlasting arms of God our Father. Even the devil acknowledged this support in the temptations of Christ in the wilderness. 'If you are the Son of God' he said 'throw yourself down; for scripture says: He will put you in his angels' charge, and they will support you on their hands in case you hurt your foot against a stone' (Matt. 4:6).

The devil does not pay compliments easily to God. The psalmist too reminds us about our relationship with God:

I love you, Yahweh, my strength
(my saviour, you rescue me from violence.)
Yahweh is my rock and my bastion,
my deliverer is my God.
I take shelter in him, my rock,
my shield, my horn of salvation,
my stronghold and my refuge.
From violence you rescue me.
He is to be praised; on Yahweh I call
and am saved from my enemies.

(Ps. 18:1–3)

We have no need to be afraid of what we may find deep
within ourselves. Whatever it is and however repulsive it
may seem to us, it is *already redeemed*. Unless we forgive
ourselves then how can we pray in the Lord's Prayer:
'Forgive us our trespasses as we forgive those who tres-
pass against us'? If we are not merciful with ourselves,
then we will mete out justice and vengeance to other
people. We have been forgiven and have experienced
God's forgiveness. In the knowledge that we are damaged people who have been healed and are being healed
by God's love, we can go out to others in gratitude and
mercy. We too often look on this phrase of the Lord's
Prayer – forgive us as we forgive others – as if we were
appealing to God's justice instead of his mercy. 'If justice
were our plea then none of us would see salvation.'

The knowledge of God's mercy to us opens up his
healing grace to others through us and we become
instruments of his peace. Bertrand Russell reminds us
that 'a man cannot possibly be at peace with others until
he has learned to be at peace with himself'. So we have
to learn to live with and by the fact that God loves us
with his love; God's love for us rather than our love of
self. This is the measure of our love for ourselves. I know
it is easier said than done but, until we begin to act in the
light of that great truth, we will never come alive. Many

psychiatrists openly admit that their work load would be drastically reduced if people had a healthy love of themselves instead of hating themselves and having guilt complexes about it.

If we feel that we are no good to anyone, least of all to ourselves, then we are in reality saying to God, 'I am sorry that you made me'. If he made us the way we are, then he had a purpose so we had better start right now in learning to live with ourselves. After all, we will have to live with ourselves in eternity. If I do not love myself, then I can love no one else. Our attitude towards others is conditioned by our attitude towards ourselves. When we do not love ourselves, then we cannot love God because we find no reason in ourselves for loving him. What we have to do is to see God at work within us 'loving us better' every moment of every day.

There is a well-known story about God puzzling as to where he would put his image in our world. He decided against putting it on the top of the highest mountain because man would be fascinated by scaling heights and, when he found God's image, he might be too engrossed in his mountaineering feats to appreciate its beauty. He decided likewise against putting it in the depths of the ocean. Finally he said: 'I shall put it in the heart of every man. He will never think of looking for it there. But if he does and finds it he will realize what a treasure he has within himself.' The kingdom of God is indeed within us and we are the temples of the Holy Spirit. God is one with us in Christ. We have his Holy Spirit praying in and for us. We are no longer orphans but God's beloved children.

We are often told that 'hell is ourselves' or that 'we make our own hell'. Yet God made us for heaven and not for hell. We were created to live at peace with ourselves so that from this peace we could reach out to the source of peace. We need to say every morning at our prayer: 'Lord, I am glad I'm me and I don't want to be anybody else. Today I am going to celebrate me and it is going to be a wonderful day. I am glad I am me because I am unique and You made me so. I am unique not only in my fingerprints but in my personality. I can only be authentic if I am myself. I believe that You see the good in me and Your love always transforms. Beauty is in the eye of the beholder and it is how You see me through the eyes of love that really matters. I want to borrow Your eyes to see myself Your way. Just as Samuel saw in David a simple shepherd boy and You saw a king so I come as a beggar to You and You clothe me with Your love. Today I shall walk tall. Yes, Lord, I'm glad I'm me.'

One of the most successful youth Masses I ever attended was celebrated by a venerable Benedictine monk who was parish priest of a large suburban parish. The feast was Christ the King and Father Damian began his introduction to the Mass with the words: 'My dear princes and princesses, today we celebrate the kingship of our brother, Jesus. We are part of a royal family.' How right he was. The reaction of the children was spontaneous. Young and old respond to love. They loved their parish priest; he loved them; they both loved God because God loved them. Love is a virtuous circle. That Mass will always remain with me as a wonderful example of the proper celebration of self.

We forget too often that God is merciful and forgives our weaknesses. In a human family the one who causes the most mischief and most worry is often the most loved. So it is with us and God. He does not love us because we are clean and shining like little Lord Fauntleroys but because we are being ourselves as he made us. We are happy to be in his presence playing like children who are often up to mischief. 'And if we are children we are heirs as well: heirs of God and coheirs with Christ, sharing his sufferings so as to share his glory' (Rom. 8:17). St. Paul reminds us: 'You are God's chosen race, his saints; he loves you' (Col. 3:12).

The authentic self tends to show through in moments when we are carried out of ourselves by strong emotions of joy or sorrow: moments when we forget who may be looking at us since it is the fear of what other people may think that often inhibits us. The dictionary defines 'to inhibit' as 'to restrain' or 'to hinder'. Martin Buber calls the devil, 'The Hinderer', the evil influence that works through our feelings of fear, doubt and discouragement to prevent us from seeing who and what we are. The devil likes us to remain displaced persons who are lost without hope of a heavenly home. He is the great destroyer of true self-love. He hinders the light of faith and love. By that light we can be liberated from the prison of fear and become whole persons.

We were meant to be fully human and to come fully alive without restrictions. That is the kind of life that God wants us to live. We are set free by the truth of Christ's saving gospel and: *'When Christ freed us, he meant us to remain free*. Stand firm therefore, and do not submit again to the yoke of slavery' (Gal. 5:1). We will enjoy the glorious liberty of the children of God, for that is who we really are. We must never allow anyone to take our heritage away from us.

God alone can change us so that we can develop our full potential as human persons and come fully alive. 'The glory of God is man fully alive,' says St Irenaeus. Yet most of us live at a tenth of our potential. We are like an iceberg with only a tenth of ourselves above the surface. So many people go through life without ever having really lived or loved. What a tragedy it is that we Christians are not filled with the sap and zest of living. We do not say a full 'yes' to life but surround our reply with 'maybe' or 'if only' or 'perhaps' or some other restricting phrase. We are conditioned people giving conditional responses when we were meant to shout 'Amen, Alleluia' to every moment of our lives in God's creation on earth.

We become instead selfish people who are never

satisfied with our lot in life. We are restless, driven on by fear that we are missing out on something. We are filled with envy of others apparently more fortunate than ourselves. The harsh truth is that we do not love ourselves. We are greedy people who amass everything except the one thing necessary for life – a love for ourselves as God loves us. A young mother told me that the most important thing for her as a mother was to love her children in their differences. In this way, she said, 'I have discovered all sorts of different love within myself of which I did not think I was capable.' God loves us to be different. We do that by being ourselves.

What makes me different? It is the still centre of my being round which my whole personality revolves. It is there deep within me where I am afraid to go. It is where God dwells within me and the devil does not want me to find it, because then I shall have found a power within myself which will destroy him. That is why I am afraid and the devil plays on my fears. I need to be released by the Spirit of the Risen Jesus so that I can come out of the dungeon of fear. Christ has come, as Isaiah foretold, to preach liberty to captives. The prison bars of self cannot contain our spirit. The resurrection of the Lord has set us free. It is his Spirit that is changing us and making us come fully alive. 'Now this Lord is the Spirit, and *where the Spirit of the Lord is, there is freedom*. And we, with our unveiled faces reflecting like mirrors the brightness of the Lord, all grow brighter and brighter as we are turned into the image that we reflect; this is the work of the Lord who is Spirit' (2 Cor. 3:18). It is by dying to our superficial ego that we allow the inner true self to emerge and live. That is indeed a true release of our spirit in union with the Spirit of the Risen Lord.

Jesus describes his true disciple in these words: 'Therefore, everyone who listens to these words of mine and acts on them will be like a sensible man who built his house on rock. Rain came down, floods rose, gales blew and hurled themselves against that house, and it did not fall: it was founded on rock' (Matt. 7:24–5).

We dig deep into ourselves and in the deep caverns we find untold treasures. It reminds me of the art of 'potholing', so popular in Yorkshire when, after long weary hours squeezing through narrow entrances, and scaling down sheer faces of underground cliffs, we come upon caves of unique beauty never before seen by anyone else. Self-discovery is the greatest possible exploration we can ever undertake. Its beauty lies in the fact that it is never-ending and ever-rewarding. It will take us a lifetime and in the process bring us life.

We undertake this search for the mystery of self in faith, believing and trusting that God will help us to overcome the barriers which separate us from our true selves. We are always changing. We will come constantly to new and exciting discoveries of what hidden and wonderful depths there are within us. We cannot perform this task alone. Christ discovers within and with us the new self, so that indeed we are converted to the Father and begin to live a new life: 'For anyone who is in Christ, there is a new creation; the old creation has gone, and now the new one is here. It is all God's work. It was God who reconciled us to himself through Christ . . .' (2 Cor. 5:17–18). The more fully we accept ourselves the more successfully we can allow and want ourselves to be changed for the better. Change is a slow and often painful process and therefore we must be patient with ourselves. '. . . we groan and find it a burden being still in this tent, not that we want to strip it off, but to put the second garment over it and to have what must die taken up into life. This is the purpose for which God made us, and he has given us the pledge of the Spirit' (2 Cor. 5:4–5).

Self-acceptance therefore does not mean that we remain, as we are, in a static state. Our faith gives us new horizons. Our hope gives us the patience to endure any hardships or setbacks we may have to suffer, but it is our love which takes us closer to God and ourselves because of its power and penetrating force. We can do more things attracted by love than we could if we were motivated by fear. One of the saddest events in my life as a priest is the memory of a person who was an alcoholic. He was aware of what his increasing bouts of drinking were doing to his wife, family and himself. He felt he could never change. Haunted by fear he took his own life in a moment of despondency. He forgot to concentrate on his love for his family and their love for him. In a sense if we really thought we could never change we would be guilty of spiritual suicide. 'I can do all things in Him who lives in me' is our gospel banner which we unfurl when the battle for self is at its fiercest.

God will piece together all the fragments of our lives, even the most negative ones, if only we have faith in him. We do not understand it now but we will one day. The harshest parts of my life in which I suffered through lack of vision in and trust by others have been the very breakwaters which guided my life in a different direction. Such people are today in my prayers since they were just the salt I needed. I see now that without their knowing it they were God's pruning knife and I am grateful for what they did to my growth as a person. There is a divine explanation for such happenings in our lives. All things conspire for good for those who love the Lord and it is loving the Lord which is the important thing we have to do. Shakespeare said: 'There is no seeming evil from which some soul of goodness may not be distilled.'

In my early days in a seminary where I was preparing for the priesthood I tried frenetically and anxiously to become less sinful and more perfect. I fell into the trap of the Stoics and punished myself too hard. I believed that everything was up to me. Self-conquest rather than self-discovery was my goal and I thought that God was leaving me on my own to get on with it. When I reached a certain stage he would take over. With this mentality I did not, of course, get very far. Years of living with the Lord have, I hope, brought more wisdom. Now I know that left to ourselves we can achieve little in the way of perfection. God changes us and he does it his way so we have to be like servants waiting on the Lord. His Spirit will show us the way and give us the means. St Paul reminds us what our attitude should be:

> I am no longer trying for perfection by my own efforts, the perfection that comes from the Law, but I want only the perfection that comes through faith in Christ, and is from God and based on faith. All I want is to know Christ and the power of his resurrection and to share his sufferings by reproducing the pattern of his death. That is the way I can hope to take my place in the resurrection of the dead. Not that I have become perfect yet: I have not yet won, but I am still running, trying to capture the prize for which Christ Jesus captured me. I can assure you my brothers, I am far from thinking that I have already won. All I can say is that I forget the past and I strain ahead for what is still to come. (Phil. 3:9–12)

We live one day at a time remembering Christ's words 'that each day has enough troubles of its own' (Matt. 6:34). We change every day through Christ's power working in us. We Christians are people of the 'now'. What we do not achieve in this life God will bring to perfection in the next. So we are not to worry unduly about our apparently slow progress in our journey back to the Father. We are pilgrims and some days we can manage a good day's journey; other days it will not be so good. However, we are pilgrims and so long as we keep our sights on Christ we will not go far wrong. Christ is our compass.

However painful the process of self-discovery may be,

111

we are not to treat ourselves as hospital patients, even though we freely acknowledge that we are weakened by the effects of sin. We rejoice in our rehabilitation since a gloomy Christian is a contradiction in terms. Happiness is like a butterfly. It eludes us when we try to grasp it but, when we sit quietly and are at peace, it comes and rests gently on our shoulder.

We recover our youth as we discover our real selves. Age is a question of attitude and outlook. The young at heart are always joyful in the Lord. They are forever young since it is the Lord who gives joy to their youth. I cannot for example resist skimming stones over the water whenever I go to the seaside. When people tell me to be my age I remind them that David danced for sheer joy before the Ark of the Covenant. Love makes us do silly things in the eyes of the world. We never really grow up because we are like fresh bread straight from the Lord's bakery. We smell of his freshness, and the world would be a better place if it had the unique aroma of fresh bread, instead of the stale smell of drab gloom and doom.

We change through love: love of God, of others and of ourselves. When people are in love then everything takes on a new dimension. Words, places, things are all different. They sparkle with God's dew, fresh every morning. Whenever I worry about the way the institutional Church is going I visit Father John, an old priest, in his late eighties. He loves the changes in the liturgy with all the enthusiasm with which he cherishes the great traditions of the past. He is a priest for all seasons and reminds me: 'Young man, remember it is God's church, and not yours.' May the Lord preserve us from the 'ecclesiastical stoop' of those who think that everything depends on their judgement. They have forgotten how to laugh and for them heaven will be a letting down of their burdens, which were not theirs in the first place! They have taken themselves too seriously and think the decisions as regards the future of the Church depend on them alone. Father John's life-style is a sermon of sheer joy. He is so in love with the Lord that he wakes up every morning looking forward to what the day will bring. Self-discovery undertaken in love and trust will bring back our youth and our joy. Father John is really alive and is a perfect example of a fully human person. Nothing disturbs him and he is quite oblivious of the influence he has on me and those with whom he comes in contact. He is my Pope John XXIII. He will never convert the world but he is renewing himself every day and therefore his world. That is all the greatest of us can ever hope to do.

In order to accept ourselves in love, we have to accept our family and its circumstances. So many people pretend that their background is different from what it really is. They conjure up a dream world in which the cottage in which they were born becomes a stately mansion and their parents were of the nobility. This is amusing if it were not so tragic. Such people never really fit into society since they are always trying to impress others by their games of make-believe. In rejecting their families they reject themselves and have cut out of their lives an area of growth.

A professor in a university in the Midlands always brings his father down to the official opening of the academic year. His father, a carpenter, wearing his ordinary ill-fitting clothes, is obviously uncomfortable in a collar and tie. His broad Yorkshire accent is music to the many professors who look forward to his annual visit, and his son is obviously very proud of him. A minority of the faculty ignore the old gentleman, but one suspects that the fault lies in them more than in anyone else. In the same way, when we love the members of our family for what they are, we are really loving ourselves. Rich or poor, we are all God's children and he loves us. Jesus was a 'commoner' who never forgot his poor origins even when dining at the rich man's table. It was the rich man who forgot the courtesies which were supplied by a woman of the streets.

Finally, since we are Christ's brothers and sisters, part of his family, he is not ashamed of any of us. 'You did not choose me, no, I chose you; and commissioned you to go out and to bear fruit, fruit that will last' (John 15:16). It is, I keep repeating, disastrous to our human growth as persons if we fail to face up to ourselves as we really are. We have to take off the masks and stop playing charades. Our real faces will take some getting used to, but they are now exposed to the life-giving rays of faith that God is our Father who loves us as we are; the thrill of hope that he believes we can change and the warmth of love which sees beyond blemishes to the true genuine worth of me as a person. At the true centre of the real me I find myself in 'Another' who loves me so that, when I turn inwards, I discover love not hate, acceptance not rejection. Previously in looking for love I searched outside myself in the world. Yet when I turn inwards I find the irreplaceable love which was always there in all my searching. In seeking the embrace of God as a loving Father I discover that I have first of all to love myself. That is what he wants. I want it too.

7. Why are you afraid to make friends?

We are afraid to love because we are afraid to let go of self. Selflessness is the price of true love which we are not prepared to pay. All human beings fear to love because to be human is to be vulnerable which means that we are subject to pain and loss. Fear of the unknown in love and what is involved is an element which is destructive of human growth. It is through people and things which we love and are afraid to lose that we lay ourselves open to hurt. The best course to follow therefore in self-defence in order to avoid pain is not to bare oneself to the cutting knife of love. What an appalling waste of life! Yet there are countless millions who follow this arid philosophy. They are the 'prisoners' whom the gospel of 'dying to self' will really set free.

Probably we will never be totally free from fear since it is such a basic emotion in our flawed humanity. When we love anyone, because of the limitations of human love we feel anxiety lest trouble, sickness and death afflict them. In them we suffer vicariously. Love breeds compassion, which means suffering with others, and if we dare to love we must be prepared to suffer. I have never 'officiated' – what a dreadful word – at a funeral without weeping inside for those who stand round the grave of their loved one. Bits of me fly off to others and through

115

them I am increased not decreased. In my own life I know from experience that those who are my close friends are the ones who have the unique power to wound and heal in a special way. Love is for brave people. It is indeed an agony as well as an ecstasy.

There is no painless way of loving but there is no other way of growing. An adolescent will never blossom to maturity unless his pillow knows the soft rain of his tears because of someone to whom he has reached out in love and who has ignored his outstretched hands. Others will never know that through them we experienced a dying and a growing. We will never be the same again, since we will go forward on the road to loving or retire behind our wounds resolved never to love again. Each encounter in love is a step forwards or backwards in our emotional growth. Love cannot stand still.

God said: 'It is not good for the man to be alone' (Gen. 2:18). A person who lives for himself alone is not fully living. As long as he excludes even one person from his life and love, he is to that degree of exclusion a lesser person. It is absolutely true that 'in giving we receive'. Love is like money. Keep it to yourself and the only future it has is to decrease in value: invest it and it will grow even as you sleep. Selfish love is of its nature self-destructive. So if we really love ourselves in the best sense of the word, then we need to look not only deeply inside ourselves but outside ourselves to find others to love. We live in a world which is thirsting for genuine love, so why not start loving today and discover what a power you have within yourself for your world? Love is a rare and precious commodity but we have made it scarce, because everyone is storing it up within themselves and refusing to let it flow out to those around us.

Buber says that man becomes 'I' through 'you'. The more I love others and give myself to them, the more I become myself. I lose nothing in the giving but, in the very process of losing myself in other people, the more I

116

discover who I really am. Life is a continuing journey of self-exploration and discovery in the world of people. I, without wanting it, shall receive from others in the measure in which I give to them. True love never thinks of receiving anything in return. Yet I shall receive even more than I give, because the generous love of just one person for me will repay all the rebuffs I might suffer from others. It is the quality rather than the quantity of love that counts. The greatest example of loving totally is Jesus who is often called 'the man for others'. He loved selflessly. That is what it means to be a Christian. Christianity is all about loving: if it is not that, then it is nothing. We will soon realize, when we try to love as Jesus did, that love of others is the heart beat which gives life blood to the proper love of self. We will discover within ourselves an inexhaustible source of loving people for their own sake. We will then love as Jesus did.

During a retreat which I gave to missioners in Africa, a middle-aged priest admitted to me that he never really loved anyone because he was afraid of being rejected. He said life for him was sheer misery since he kept everyone at arms' length from his affection and confidence. He had, as it were, a large sign placed in front of him: 'Trespassers will be prosecuted!' He had become a professional dispenser of sacraments – a human slot machine. He took consolation in performing his tasks with great care and attention to detail so that everything went according to the book. He never saw people as individuals to love but only in terms of how they stood with regard to the discipline of the Church. His parishioners respected him but few loved him because he would not allow them to get to know him. He did not really love himself and saw God as a just judge who would scrutinize every iota of his life. He was afraid of losing his vocation as a priest if he drew too close to others. Yet he was destroying his priestly ministry by his refusal to let go and trust the Lord. We laid hands on him in the healing

117

ministry and now he is a different person. He is released for loving and sharing himself with others.

Love approaches creation when we reach out to other people in order to *make contact*. In the depth of our being, when we listen to love's cry longing for fulfilment, we know we are not meant to live for ourselves alone. Shut in on ourselves we will die. Michelangelo's painting in the Sistine Chapel of the creation of man depicts God reaching out to man so that the tips of their fingers meet: God from his world makes contact with man in his. Deep inside each one of us there is a power created for love. It is hidden in the inner recesses of our personality and I like to call it the 'power-house of life and love'. Many people lock the door which leads to that inner power-house and so for them the great dynamo of love never comes to life.

It needs someone other than ourselves to set that dynamo in action. We have to trust ourselves to them but sometimes we are not prepared to take the risk. So if the dynamo of love within us is never set in motion, we will never know what it would have been like if we were to come ablaze with light. Even though we have this most powerful system of lighting within us, we make do with candles and even these we hide so that we walk through life in darkness. Soon we will return to cursing the darkness when eventually the candle goes out. When Jesus told us we were the light of the world he was issuing us with the challenge 'to love and let go'. Why is it that so few are prepared to accept that challenge to 'love the world better'? We were made to love: God, ourselves and others so that time not spent in loving is time wasted. Love will always get through when everything else fails. What a shame that some Christians have an inner room in their deepest being where everything is gathering dust and falling into decay. We become people who are shrivelled up inside since nothing grows in darkness.

Many people in today's world have an inner, loveless

118

emptiness. Human love at its deepest level is never allowed to enter this secret desolate place. People forget that Jesus says to them: 'Behold, I stand at the door and knock. If anyone hears my voice and opens the door I will go in and sup with him and he with me' (Rev. 3:20). In the depths of their being lonely people hear the call, but they are afraid to answer because of the consequences involved. From now on, once they love and are loved, they will no longer be alone and self is lost. Yet the only thing they will lose in love is their loneliness.

Lonely people are sad inside even though on the outside they may smile and look happy. They weep tears of the soul. They turn outwards to answer the cry that comes from deep within. They stop their ears and run away from the closed door, until the knocking becomes an ever-decreasing background sound lost in the useless noise of a world which will not allow them to listen to themselves. They enact a modern 'Hound of Heaven' as they run away from the God in themselves which they discover through other people. They may have a lot of money, security and all the world has to offer but in themselves they are empty. The bitter wind of loneliness blows through their lives chilling them in their innermost being. They are afraid of getting old and being left alone. They become today's Midas regretting that they ever asked for the power of the golden touch.

In recent months I have conducted a phone-in on the radio through which people talk to me about their problems. I have been overwhelmed by the loneliness and lack of love in our materialistic world. People seem to have everything but love. They want to be told that they are loved and wanted for themselves and not for what they have or what they do.

Today people need to reach out and touch their neighbour so that they will not feel alone, yet they are afraid to take the initiative. We need to touch them – to make contact – as someone who is near on whom they can lean.

Now I know how burdened Jesus was with the cares of a world which longed to be healed. People came pressing round him to touch even the hem of his garment since the power of love went out from him.

We Christians have a great apostolate to today's nomadic people who want to put down roots in the soil of love. When we reach out to them we lose ourselves in order that in Christ we may together with them find God as a loving Father. The world cries out to us in the silence of the night. We know that God is where their dreams are. He is in the depths of their personality but they need someone to help them in their search. This is exactly what Jesus did.

The Incarnation – God coming to us as man – means not only that God came offering his friendship in the flesh and blood of Jesus, but that people find God especially through the love and friendship of other people. The words of Jesus have a meaning for every age: 'For where two or three meet in my name, I shall be there with them' (Matt. 18:20). These words ring out even clearer today. Our world is lonely and dark. People who walk in darkness need to touch someone who can see so that together they can find the way out into the sunlight. The light we are guided by is the light of love. Jesus will always be the only way. Love is a commandment as old yet as fresh as the Christian message itself. Listen to St John:

My dear people
this is not a new commandment that I am writing to tell you, but *an old commandment*
that you were given from the beginning,
the original commandment which was the message brought to you.
Yet in another way, what I am writing to you,
and what is being carried out in your lives as it was in his,
is a new commandment;

120

because the night is over
and the real light is already shining.
Anyone who claims to be in the light
but hates his brother
is still in the dark.
But anyone who loves his brother is living in the light
and need not be afraid of stumbling.

(1 John 2:7–9)

We are Christ's brothers for other people, the 'friends of the world':

If you refuse to love, you must remain dead;
to hate your brother is to be a murderer,
and murderers, as you know, do not have eternal life
in them.
This has taught us love –
that he gave up his life for us;
and we, too, ought to give up our lives for our
brothers.
If a man who was rich enough in this world's goods
saw that one of his brothers was in need,
but closed his heart to him,
how could the love of God be living in him?
My children,
our love is not just words or mere talk,
but something real and active.

(1 John 3:15–18)

People today seem lonelier than ever before. As man walks on the moon, people's eyes search even further afield for an answer to the problems they feel deep inside. At the same time that man is conquering nature and making it give up its secrets he is even more puzzled by the mysterious cleavage within himself. The loneliness in people's hearts today is their inability to find God because they are too distracted to look inside themselves.

121

People ask, is God a reality or a myth? If they do not believe in him, however desperately they try, perhaps it is because fundamentally they do not believe in themselves or in others. Yet they will want him if we show them that he is alive in our lives. We are the witnesses of a love which the world cannot live without. Today there is the shattering silence of loneliness, even within marriage, because husbands and wives cannot give each other what is deeper than themselves. They feel cheated because they invested their happiness in another person, forgetting that no one can bring us fulfilment unless we are prepared to accept its discovery within ourselves. We are not to live by shortened horizons. God made us for himself and nothing short of that vision will suffice. If we can show that the source of our happiness is God, then those with whom we come into loving contact will begin to believe in him as well as believing in themselves.

Our love for people helps them to love themselves. God uses us to help him to heal his wounded world since we are our brother's keepers. That is the wonderful trust God places in us. We are good Christians in so far as we help to restore other people to wholeness. We who are strengthened by experiencing God's healing power are bound to help the weak so that, like war-wounded on a long march, we offer a helping shoulder on which the less fortunate can lean. The whole of my ministry as a priest has been directed to that end. The value of the priesthood for me is not in the administration of the sacraments independent of people, but in the concern which we have for people at a human level, which reaches its climax when they receive the sacraments as signs of God's special love for them manifested through caring people. We are ambassadors of God's love. Even though God alone can bring them to wholeness, we as Christians are his invitation to them to open their hearts through our visible caring and sharing of their lives. We are God's mirror for other people so that they can see their real value in our eyes as another loving, caring human person.

Christian love makes people come alive in much the same way as human love between two people who discover that they are meant for each other's completeness. We can all give myriad examples of this from our own lives. There is one story which I would like to share with you since it is a very special one. Eight years ago Mother Teresa of Calcutta decided to speak at Leeds but as usual she gave very short notice. It was impossible to find a suitable hall to accommodate the people who would come to hear her. There was no time to organize the necessary advertising but the name Mother Teresa has a magical ring all of its own. I offered our centre at Wood Hall and it was packed with people of all ages from every walk of life. She spoke quite simply of the spiritual hunger for love in those we meet if only we look at people as our brothers and sisters in Christ. At the end of her talk she went round our conference hall and spoke individually to each person, young and old. One person there, whom I had been trying to help spiritually for years had his life transformed by what she said to him. When I asked what she said he replied, 'God love and bless you.' 'But', I said, 'I have been saying that to you for years.' He replied with a smile, 'She said it with all her being and I realized that God was so real to her that he came alive for me.'

Mother Teresa has this special gift of radiating God's love, but we can all do it each in our own individual way. Mother Teresa lets God come through and that is why the world loves her. She helps to activate people's love for God because she is so obviously God-activated herself. Love is very contagious once we catch the germ ourselves. When a priest loves his people they can no longer be indifferent to his message. I have found that sharing people's moments of great joy or deep sorrow has been the launching pad by which with them I have discovered the greatness of God's love.

When we offer love or friendship to others we do so in order to set them free to live their lives as whole persons. In this way we are healing them. Healing leads to wholeness and the measure of our lives as Christians is the number of people who owe their wholeness to our loving, selfless care. I can never understand why we are told that we are not to get involved with people; as if God distrusts all forms of human friendship. Without meaning to, we are subconsciously saying that all friendship has illicit sexual overtones. Freud has become our mentor and not Jesus who publicly mixed with the sinners and drop-outs of his world. Thomas à Kempis wrote in *The Imitation of Christ* that the more he went out among men the less he came back as a man. I know what he meant, because he was a very holy person, but in my more facetious moments I wonder whom he met and what he did once he was outside his monastery! If my fear of the world is dominated by a distrust of emotional involvement, then I shall never never really trust anyone, least of all myself.

It is this lack of trust which is one of the most destroying elements in the life of the institutional Church. If the institution does not trust me, then I am being taught not to trust those within it. In this way we Christians distrust each other and the devil makes mayhem of all our ideals. The institution that does not live and preach trust condemns itself in the light of Christ's gospel. *Ubi caritas et amor, Deus ibi est*. 'Where love and trust abide, there is God.' Love and trust are two sides of the one coin. The early Christians were known by their love rather than by their efficiency and bureaucratic government. The institutional Church when it trusts me heals me in a way that its rules never could. Rules are too hygienic and sterile for human growth. The loving doctor heals his patient so that he can lead as full a life as possible in the world outside the hospital. The Church heals and helps me for my life in the world. This may be a wicked world but our lives should redeem it. St Paul prayed for the Philippians that they might be 'innocent and genuine, perfect children of God among a deceitful and underhand brood, and you will shine in the world like bright stars. . . .' (Phil. 2:14).

Our loving contact with others gives them the power to love themselves by nourishing in them a true sense of their own worth in their own eyes. For them life really becomes worth living since love transforms life. When I offer my friendship to someone I am saying in fact: 'I am your friend with no strings attached. It does not matter what you do or have done. My friendship is unconditional for you as a person. I want to be always there with you whether you need me or not. Don't ask me why. Just be happy, as I am, that I value your friendship as something very important in my life. I commit myself to you so that my life is fuller because of our friendship.'

Christ died and rose from death to give life to everyone. It is on Christians especially that the obligation lies to bear witness to this selfless form of loving friendship. We offer friendship to others because Christ offered it to us first. Friendship is only kept when it is shared. Never mind what other people do. Our standards are set by Christ himself and that is the vision we keep before our eyes.

True love, and every friendship is a form of love, always liberates without ever becoming possessive. We give to our friends the freedom to be themselves so they never feel used or manipulated. We affirm the other as 'other' when we allow him to grow to maturity in his own individual way. No one person or group belongs to us. Too often we wish people to be the kind of people we want them to be rather than the people they want to be themselves. Just as the doctor wants his son to follow in his footsteps in medicine, many Christians quite blatantly put joining their denomination before a deep sensitive consideration of the feelings of the individual they wish to help. They are ecclesiastical head-hunters who are satisfied with nominal allegiance rather than the deep conviction of faith.

Organizations and institutions which are bent on self-preservation have a rigid system which demands uniformity. They regard loyalty as the supremely essential quality required of their followers. Such systems destroy the individual and substitute the primacy of law for love. They run contrary to the gospel teaching of man's individuality in the realm of conscience. They forget that God himself respects man's freedom. People are very much afraid, therefore, of being manipulated even by the Church: of being wanted for what they can give rather than what they are in themselves. They are apprehensive lest they are being used or exploited.

Let me give you an example. Recently I helped a young refugee family from Northern Ireland settle in Yorkshire. They had been through the traumatic experience of having their lives threatened in Belfast and being forced to flee their country with no money or spare clothing. A supportive group of Christians of all denominations which I had formed gave them all the necessary help we could muster. A house was put at their disposal, then furniture, bedding, clothes and all the essential requirements for a home appeared as if by magic. The children were settled in and I found a job for the emotionally shattered father. Within a few weeks a pentecostal group visited the family, presuming they were easy prey, and welcomed them along to their church. They appeared to be friendly but when the family did not turn up for service on the following Sunday they were promptly dropped. The angry parents demanded of me: 'Why did they come?' but they and I both knew the answer. Proselytizers are interested in systems not people. As Christians we are interested in people for their own sake. It is our privilege and duty to help, whatever the outcome.

True caring for the other in friendship means that I want the other to become his best self according to his own insights and vision. My friendship unlocks the door for him and sets him free to find others to love and to be loved by. I may never see him again or have the same close union with him, but I shall be pleased that God has used me to turn the key that unlocked his prison cell. One of my favourite films, 'Born Free', is of a young lioness which was reared by a gamekeeper and his wife and when the animal was sufficiently strong it was let loose to live its own life in the natural setting of the jungle.

We are all born free and God wants us to remain so. No one belongs to another. There are no slaves in our world and that is why human rights are written into the heart of our personality. We must not manipulate others for our own satisfaction just as we naturally throw off the shackles with which others would bind us. The Church that in practice as well as theory proclaims the unassailable dignity of the individual will have the world listening to its authentic voice. It will have many enemies because there is a cannibal instinct in man to possess others rather than free them.

When we meet another in a deep encounter we say I want to become 'your friend' rather than for you to be 'my friend'. This means that I want what is best for you. I want to set you free to be yourself, to become fully alive. I am sensitive to your value as a unique part of the mystery and glory of God's world. I do not desire to become your whole life for your horizons may differ from mine. My wish is for you to experience all the joys of your world and in your happiness I too find happiness. You owe me nothing and if you can say 'I am glad I am me' then your difference from me in many things does not in any way threaten our friendship. We have helped each other to come alive and for this I praise the Lord. He alone is your world and mine!

When we share a deep friendship with another we are communicating at various levels of our personality. Sometimes we give more to another than they are prepared to give back in return. That does not matter. If only we could see into the future we would be amazed at the hidden influences for good we have on other people's lives and they on ours. Frightened people give little just because they are afraid. They will come out of their burrows like rabbits, timid at first but gradually they will play in the open fields in the sunlight knowing they have nothing to fear. Our world is startlingly full of frightened people who do not want to be hurt any more. People hurt each other, so what reason have they for trusting us? They are damaged people who are in a sense society's lepers. They still need caring for like the leper who cried out to Jesus, 'Sir . . . if you want to you can cure me.' Jesus said, 'Of course I want to! Be cured!' (Luke 5:13).

People are prepared to be open about themselves in moments of great joy or deep sorrow. At times of crisis they are less able to put their masks on and it is at these times that we have the opportunity of getting through their defence barriers. Priests are in a unique position to help people discover themselves, since every parish or community has a built-in mechanism of turning to the clergy when grief is just round the corner.

I have spent hours with damaged people of many faiths and none. Some have obviously manipulated me by using me as a vehicle on which to vent their anger and suppressed emotions. They never come near me except when they are in trouble. The sound of their names conjures up long hours of tears and tirades leaving them self-satisfied and me an emotional wet rag. Such people are incapable of love or friendship, and look for reasons for their loneliness outside themselves. The priest is a convenient whipping boy and that is as it should be. I have become their crutch but some day, please God, I shall become their key. As Christian healers in a dam-

128

aged world we do not always deal with success stories. Like the Master we are sent to the lost sheep who bleat pitifully on the precarious mountain ledges of their own making. Who will carry them on their shoulders if we ignore them?

The most precious gift we can give to another is 'availability of self'. That is one quality for whose lack of use we can all strike our breasts. We excuse ourselves by saying we are 'too tired', 'no, not again', or 'my goodness, don't people realize I have a life of my own'. Yet when I make myself available to another I am saying: 'I am listening to you now. Forget how long it takes. You just tell me about yourself in your own way and at your own pace. I don't want to be anywhere else but here with you. You are my world and its centre is you. Let me be the mirror in which you can see yourself perhaps clearer than before. My mind and heart are with you because I want desperately to feel what you feel. I want to make contact with you so that you can make contact with yourself.' In this process of dialogue, during which I may say nothing, I come across a new discovery of myself in another in which the damaged person becomes my mirror in which I see my own imperfections. It is a case of 'physician heal thyself'. The discoveries in medicine depend on the illnesses of patients. It is the same with Christian healing. We are healed by those who come to us for healing.

An illustration of 'listening in depth' is that of a young father who had just been told that he was critically ill with cancer, and I was asked to visit him. We had met only once before. As I entered the ward I found him lying on his bed looking at the ceiling in fear and disbelief at what had overtaken him. I sat there and asked him to tell me about his worries. No drugs seemed to bring him rest so I took his hand in mine and projected myself into his situation. Soon I saw myself in him and in some inexplicable way I was experiencing to some degree his emotions.

129

Together we came through his crisis point and I felt closer to him than if we had been life-long friends. We had both experienced a beautiful and unique situation. I visited him many times on subsequent days and discovered a peace within him which I knew I did not give. It was God's peace conveyed through me. His attitude to life deepened, not in the sense that he was not a good person already, but that he saw everything in a new and wonderful way. At his request, in the presence of his wife and closest friends, I received him into the Church. How or why this happened to and through me I shall never know. I suppose it is one of the almond blossoms or snow-drops that the Lord strews in our path as pilgrims to cheer the winter days.

I can only 'listen authentically' to another when I am not afraid to give myself totally to him. If I hold back anything of myself which I am not prepared to reveal, then to that extent I am not listening. There is no real dialogue, no listening and I am engaging in the 'conversation of the deaf' where *people talk at each other* without ever really listening to what the other is saying. Jesus said, 'blessed are the ears that hear what you hear' meaning that we are blessed if we listen with our hearts as well as our heads. In that way we *talk to each other*; heart to heart; deep to deep. The more of ourselves we are prepared to reveal, the more we encourage others to be themselves in honest dialogue. We see behind the words and gestures to the person of the speaker. If ever there is a hush when we enter a room, it may well be a sign that people have to switch off conversation and begin telling me the things I want to hear. They do not want to upset me so they tell me how gorgeous my splendid attire is, even though they know I am naked. In secret they resent the violence done to truth and to their integrity as real persons.

When I tell you by my attitude that 'I am listening', I am really saying 'I love you; I am your friend. You are

130

not alone. We are together as one. What you feel, I feel. I have taken a risk in letting you know who I am and you have done the same for me. Thank you for helping me by allowing me to help you. What we have shared is something precious to us both.'

We need to be more truthful. The devil is the father of lies and no one wants to live a lie. The more a person is open to himself, the more he is open to God. The Christian in love with God as a Father who cares for everyone can really help others come alive. God comes to people and we are the 'incarnation' of his love whenever we make him visible to others through our loving care and compassion. That is our mission and responsibility. Gradually the message will dawn like a new day and those we have loved will walk in the sunlight. We will share with them a renewed awareness of God's love. Even though only he can make them fully human and fully alive, nevertheless we will have shared with him in the joy of the Resurrection of one who was dead and has come to life again. God has touched us as friends and together we leave the valley of the darkness of fear.